·LA VIE·
PARISIENNE

A Good Café
on the Place St-Michel

©2004 Cavallini Papers & Co., Inc. - Printed

Velours toujou

spendue

·LA VIE·
PARISIENNE

LOOKING FOR LOVE–
AND THE PERFECT LINGERIE

Janelle McCulloch

PIER
9

For my five nieces, Alex, Meg, Gemma,
Shae and Abbey Wiedermann,
who would love Paris with a passion.

And for my parents,
Ross and Jenny Wiedermann,
who don't realise I've been to Paris
far more than I may have let on ...

It's all here in
BLACK &
WHITE

First published in 2008 by Pier 9, an imprint of
Murdoch Books Pty Limited

Murdoch Books Australia
Pier 8/9
23 Hickson Road
Millers Point NSW 2000
Phone: +61 (0)2 8220 2000
Fax: +61 (0)2 8220 2558
www.murdochbooks.com.au

Murdoch Books UK Limited
Erico House, 6th Floor
93–99 Upper Richmond Road
Putney, London SW15 2TG
Phone: +44 (0) 20 8785 5995
Fax: +44 (0) 20 8785 5985
www.murdochbooks.co.uk

Chief Executive: Juliet Rogers
Publishing Director: Kay Scarlett

Editorial Manager: Colette Vella
Editors: Karen Ward and Ali Lavau
Design: Gayna Murphy
Photography: Janelle McCulloch
Production: Monique Layt

National Library of Australia Cataloguing-in-
Publication Data:

McCulloch, Janelle.
La vie Parisienne : looking for love and the perfect
lingerie.

ISBN 9781741960822 (pbk.).

1. McCulloch, Janelle. 2. Journalists - Australia -
Biography. 3. Paris (France) - Description and travel.
4. Paris (France) - Social life and customs. I. Title.

070.92

A catalogue record for this book is available from the
British Library.

Printed by Hang Tai Printing Company Limited
in 2008. PRINTED IN CHINA.

PARIS

J'AIME LA V...

CHANEL THE COUTU...

Karl Lagerfeld

la hume la hume la hume la h

Par...

es
...ith
...cen

...ee
...arr

...TING
...YLING
...PR

open

TARIF PLEIN
Guichet www.fondation-pb-ysl.net   NO BILLE
Edite le : 05/01/2006 11:06 PUBLI

Whoever does not visit
Paris regularly will never
really be elegant.

Honoré de Balzac, 1815

. 1 .

Martinis and Macaroons

THE MAGIC OF FOREIGN ROMANCES

Paris is always a good idea.

Audrey Hepburn in *Sabrina*

In my favourite Paris neighbourhood, the famously romantic sixth arrondissement on the grand Left Bank, there is a ravishing pastry shop called Ladurée. You may have already heard of it, since it has passed into the realm of cult destinations to visit when you're lingering in this city, mainly because it's part tea salon and part visual feast. Beloved by everyone from fashion models to fur-wearing aristocrats, this sophisticated patisserie has become famous for many things—most of them fabulously calorific—but the one thing it's most known for is its macaroon, a dainty almond biscuit that has been elevated into a seductive work of art. Flavoured with everything from lime and ginger to bitter chocolate and even java pepper (a very Parisian shade of grey), this tiny confection has become the Chanel of desserts in Paris, thanks to Ladurée's decision to release new collections each season, just as the fashion designers do with the *haute couture* shows.

I pause here on an almost weekly basis, drawn to the windows like Holly Golightly in *Breakfast at Tiffany's*—and there are curious similarities, with Ladurée's signature mint-green boxes becoming as coveted as Tiffany & Co's duck-egg blue ones among the fashion set. (In a quirky twist, Tiffany's signature colour was supposedly inspired by Marie Antoinette's favourite shade, Nattier blue, while the 'modern' Marie Antoinette of Sofia Coppola's stylised film was inspired by Ladurée's sugary pastel shades.) I love to come to this irresistible patisserie when I want to be reminded of how beautiful Paris can be—and how even a simple macaroon can become art. Paris is like that, you see. Even the confectionery is sexy.

When I've finished gazing at perfect pastries I'll wander through lively streetscapes to the rue de Buci street market near St-Germain-des-Prés, an atmosphere-laden neighbourhood on the Left Bank that fulfils just about every fantasy you ever had about being in Paris. Here, my favourite ruddy-faced butcher and fishmonger—culinary counsellors with knobbly hands but beautiful hearts—proffer tips on how to seduce a Frenchman with a plump goose from the Périgord, before deciding that a hearty homemade soup is probably less work, and more seductive anyway. If there's time I'll stop for a hot chocolate at one of my favourite Paris bistros—crowded, century-old cafés that have thankfully retained the aura of their classic past, with wooden tables dressed in white paper and mirrors reflecting chalky blackboards and couples about to kiss. Afterwards, if it's warm, I'll make my way through Hemingway's and F. Scott Fitzgerald's old neighbourhood near the St-Sulpice cathedral to the Luxembourg Gardens and its parterres of pistachio-green chairs for a stroll among the statuary and formal gravel paths. Or I'll join other flavour-obsessed food lovers—including Catherine Deneuve, Audrey Tatou, John Galliano, Carla Bruni and Gérard Depardieu—at the organic market on leafy boulevard Raspail, where stylish Parisians fill string bags and elegant baskets with enticing limes, bundles of fresh basil, heirloom tomatoes, sleek leeks and spears so slender they could be the Kate Moss of the vegetable garden.

At the end of the day, I'll wander home through the enchanting narrow streets, full of good humour and, quite often, a little homemade cider, courtesy of a flirtatious merchant. I will have usually bought some *roquette*, a baguette, a couple of robust tomatoes and a bottle of organic Bordeaux to wash it all down with. And I will feel, as I always do in this sublime city, extremely grateful—and extraordinarily content.

This is my life in Paris, my Parisian life—or *la vie Parisienne*, as the locals say. And it's what I'd always imagined it to be. An education in style, glamour, gastronomy and grace in a place where even the asparagus spears are exquisite.

I have lingered in Paris on and off for much of my twenties and thirties. Like many raised on images of Chanel, Cartier-Bresson, Doisneau and Dior, I thought my life would be infinitely enriched if only I lived in a cramped attic studio a cork-pop from the Left Bank with a view of the Seine and an *armoire* full of French knickers and killer heels. I thought that Paris would make me glamorous, or at least educated in the art of glamour. I imagined that after an appropriate length of time in my French lover's arms (the French lover being part of the promised Paris package), I would emerge looking like Carole Bouquet or *Amélie*'s Audrey Tautou, brazenly beautiful but coolly detached and fabulously attired in something that would stop mopeds on the boulevard St-Germain. I would also be speaking in smoky tones and sexily caressing a cigarette. Even though I don't smoke. I imagined I would be sophisticated. Seductive. *Soignée*.

I was wrong, of course. It takes a lot more than style and a kiss from a Frenchman to make a woman complete, let alone content. Nevertheless, I can't help but adore this place. It is everything that I'm not, but hope to be. Most writers and journalists drift towards New York and the bright lights of Manhattan, but I have always preferred Paris. My dreams are embedded in the soft pink haze of its twilight skylines, the stately greys and champagnes of its elegant architecture, and its black-on-black-on-ivory bistros and bars, where possibilities for love lie behind every bottle of Beaujolais.

I am certainly not the first to fall in love with this city and I can't imagine I will be the last. Paris has always been the point where the world's fashion, gastronomy, design and style axes converge in an irresistible matrix of concentrated glamour.

Where else is it obligatory, as part of one's sartorial and sexual education, to buy hand-stitched, soft-as-air lingerie the colour of cognac, shoes crafted like magnificent edifices, and dresses that whisper 'kiss me' when you glide down the street? Where else can you walk home along the Seine with someone you love just as the violet twilight is falling on the city, and murmur mischievous, French-accented innuendo without feeling silly? And where else does longing hang as heavy in the air as cigarette smoke in a St-Germain bistro?

There is something about Paris, an irrepressible seductiveness that makes people feel nostalgic for things they didn't realise they wished for. It is the last guardian of glamour: a city that whispers of romance, and the promise of passion and a fabulous life.

Ironically, despite my Chanel and Cartier-Bresson obsessions, I resisted the city for the longest time. I don't know why. Perhaps, in all its glamour and grandeur, it represented something that seemed too unattainable?

Whatever the reason, a few months after graduating from university in 1994 I moved straight to London, where I eventually landed a job as a journalist on a travel magazine. I also fell in love.

It was, I remember, an enormous surprise. I never expected to encounter romance—certainly not so soon and certainly not with a gentleman who turned out to be the Queen Mother's equerry. Nevertheless, there he was. My knight in shining Armani.

We met at Baker Street tube station, at quarter to midnight two weeks before Christmas. I remember he was wearing a finely tailored black suit, a white shirt with silver cufflinks, an elegant black leather belt and a white pocket-handkerchief, all of which made him look strangely handsome at that fading hour. It was the kind of style that said 'Old London': Tony Bennett; St James's gentlemen's clubs; G&Ts at five. I fell in love at first sight.

Two days later, after three cheap wines, a just-as-cheap meal in Covent Garden and four far-from-cheap kisses by a Soho streetlamp, I was completely and utterly smitten. The rest, as they say, is nudity.

I couldn't have known he was an *homme fatal* of the worst kind.

Unlike Paris, London is and has always been a man's town. It is tailor-made (no pun intended) for men. Places like Paris are far more feminine in feel, with lines and landscapes that are as sensual as a Dior gown. But London is reserved, well and truly, for gentlemen. This is a place where you can find all manner of tweed for suiting but only two sorts of women's underwear—Marks & Spencer and Agent Provocateur. And most men here prefer the latter.

Despite their wicked ways, it's not difficult to fall for these well-dressed cads. (Although not all of them are cads, I hasten to add. Some of them are absolutely lovely. But the ones who are lovely are usually married and living a quiet life down in Hastings or Devon.) London men, by and large, are renowned for their charm and their British wit. They're smooth and rough, chivalrous and daring, old-fashioned and utterly, irresistibly dangerous, all in the same elegantly nonchalant pose. And when they stand there, flashing their silver cufflinks and asking with a wink if you'd like to join them in having 'a grown-up drink', it's hard not to fall head over Jimmy Choo heels. I tell you, London men can entice you inside like a modern Bond in an Ozwald Boateng suit.

My London Man didn't tell me what he did at first, which was perhaps wise given his sensitive role and my media connections. I merely assumed, mostly from the bespoke suits, that he worked in the City. I never bothered to ask if he mixed the Queen Mother's drinks and scheduled her day.

Then one evening, after a drink in Soho, he casually asked if I'd mind if he swung by work to pick up some papers. Of course not, I said politely, and so we proceeded to detour through the West End. Five minutes later, we were driving towards St James's Palace. I had no idea where we were going. But I could never have imagined we would end up in the royal estate.

As the navy Rover convertible sliced through the winter streets, tearing down Pall Mall and along Cleveland Row, with you-know-who whistling spiritedly in the seat beside me, I sat there quietly wringing my new dress (which I'm sure came with specific instructions 'not to wring' in fifteen languages on the label). It was only when we approached Stable Yard Road and the sentry emerged from his box and murmured, 'Good evening, sir,' that I finally knew, with sickening certainty, where we were.

I wasn't prepared for a tour of royal life that night and I certainly wasn't prepared to pass into the inner sanctum of the Queen Mother's private quarters. I thought we were simply off to some stuffy office to collect a dull file. So when he waltzed down a hall filled with photos of Princes Will and Harry, turned right into an enormous room and calmly pressed a secret button that opened a wall to reveal a private bar the size of the Royal Albert Hall, I was, for the first time in my journalistic life, completely speechless.

At the time, London was in the grip of the new Cool Britannia economy and the city was celebrating. After years of an ethos that suggested cool could only come from being dull and depressed, everyone was ready for glamour and action, including those—in fact, especially those—who worked within media and royal circles. Now media people in London are like media people anywhere: obsessed with sex, gossip and adventure. But the media crowd I was mingling with was the most obsessive, sexual and adventurous of all. Blessed with swizzle-stick figures, their idea of a perfect evening was a spoonful of white powder in one hand, a naked abdomen in the other and no pressing deadlines in between. As one food writer friend quipped to me, 'Honey, the only kind of dressing these people care about is undressing!'

During this time, cocktail frocks and dinner jackets became the new khakis for the fashion crowd, and champagne flowed from dinner until breakfast at Annabel's, which was still one of the best places for a dance and a dangerous liaison. As a friend later put it, it was an age of 'irresponsible hedonism': a fabulous, alcohol-fuelled fantasy. And my equerry and his royal duties were a dreamlike part of it.

Needless to say, I found this sanguine new society utterly mesmerising. For an Australian country girl who grew up surrounded by uninspiring ordinariness, it was a city filled with quivering possibilities. And so into this life I quietly entered and it was here I quietly stayed, desperately hoping no one evicted me for good behaviour.

I was born in a small town called Castlemaine, in western Victoria, which is famous for its antique shops, its National Trust–listed stone cottages, and Raimond Gaita, the author, philosopher and Professor of Moral Philosophy at King's College London, who wrote about

the region in his prize-winning memoir, *Romulus, My Father.* When I was three (my parents were teachers; moving was part of the career path), we moved to a town called Swan Hill, which is famous for its migrant Italian population and its magnificent food but not, strangely enough, its hills or swans. Three years later, my mother and father finally decided to settle in an area of Victoria called Gippsland, which is famous for green mountain ranges, misty weather, a great many cows and not much else. Quiet is not the word for it. It is beautiful, yes, but about the most exciting thing that happens is the leaves changing colour. It is the perfect breeding ground for dreams.

The worst thing about growing up in the country is the lack of choice, particularly when it comes to fashion. Back in the early eighties, the High Street shops carried only two kinds of jeans—denim blue and a slightly darker denim blue—and just as few styles of anything else. Even worse, all the stores closed at noon at Saturday and resolutely stayed closed the rest of the weekend, so if you wanted a new outfit for the Blue Light Disco on Saturday night to impress that cute boy whose mother taught your ballet class, well, you were all out of luck.

Little happened in this town, unless you hung around the indoor rollerskating rink (it was the eighties, remember: Cliff Richard and white skates were big), the aforementioned Blue Light Disco, the pub, the country club, the local park after the disco, and our caravan parked at the very back of my parents' property. Quite a lot happened in there. Although with my parents being teachers, most of it was above board. It was the kind of town where the dentist lived next door to the doctor who played golf with the policeman whose toddler son was in your mother's class, so you couldn't do anything—from sneaking out to a party to lighting an illicit cigarette in the old caravan—without someone finding out. Usually your father. Who was waiting back in the house with something hard from the kitchen drawer.

Country towns are agonising for young girls who read *Vogue*, long for different styles of jeans, borrow Danielle Steel novels from the library and dream of European streets and dark-eyed men in poetic black polonecks reading Proust with a French accent. The landscapes of the places you grow up in deeply affect who you are, and I couldn't wait to leave. I felt like the odd one out: the misfit, the dreamer, the proverbial square peg. While other girls longed to get married and settle down to quiet nights of bliss, I fanaticised about the thrill of moving to a city and living amid a twenty-four-hour din. I wanted the comforting clatter of traffic, police sirens and non-stop alarms to lull me to sleep, rather than a rural tranquillity that seemed to drift on forever. At the age of thirteen I decided that I didn't like the country. I didn't like all the trees and the open landscapes. They made me uneasy. Restless. The silence scared me. I used to jump on a train and travel to the city just to feel safe.

One year, a friend who was into everything equestrian invited me to go riding with her. She put me on an ex-racehorse. I can't remember its name but I'm sure it wasn't Dobbin. It had eyes like the devil and a rump so high you needed a crane to get on. Before I could put my feet in the stirrups and remember how to rise to the trot, she thwacked The Horse Who Wasn't Dobbin and the thirty-hands-high thoroughbred took off. Two kilometres down the paddock, it headed towards a lethal-looking barbed-wire fence, and made as if to jump. At that moment I knew, with the certainty of someone who is about to suffer concussion, if not death, that I was not made to live in the countryside.

And so, in my teens, I happily left the country for a school in Melbourne called St Margaret's. However, that only made the longings worse, because all of a sudden I had friends who seemed to pop off to *different* cities—far more impressive-sounding ones than Melbourne, such as London or Paris—at the drop of a beret. With their knowledge of fashion and their penchant for reading the sex pages of *Cosmo* in between all their jaunts overseas, they appeared frightfully sophisticated, even though they were still only fourteen, and all wonderfully worldly—far worldlier than a girl who had only ever worn two pairs of jeans and travelled to the Gold Coast for her holidays.

My time to travel overseas eventually came when I was fifteen and won a Rotary scholarship to study in Denmark for a year. I loved it so much I didn't want to go back to Australia again. There in Europe, among centuries-old villages wrapped in fairytale-style layers of snow, I felt as though I had finally found my spiritual home.

It took several more years before I could return for good, ostensibly as a backpacker but in my heart as a fully paid-up Europhile. But when the plane touched down at London's Gatwick airport at three am on a fog-filled, Dickensian night and I grabbed my bag and my much-thumbed copy of British *Vogue* and took a black cab to the South Kensington hotel that my father had kindly booked me into, I knew with absolute certainty that I had finally come home.

That winter in London, between November 1994 and January 1995, I spent in a kind of augmented reality. I had moved to the tiny, exquisitely beautiful, nip-and-tucked village of Brompton Cross, into the basement flat of a tall, white Victorian house with an eggshell-coloured door. My place didn't boast the topiaried splendour of the other temples to architecture in this des. res. corner of the city, and my flat was barely bigger than a post-it note, but I did have a window looking out to an overgrown garden and another to an inner courtyard, where the pigeons used to poo.

I couldn't believe I was in Europe, let along dating an equerry to the British royal family. A former Irish Guards officer who had been in the Gulf War, my boyfriend was primarily a glorified PA—albeit a dashing, well-dressed one who could make a knockout G&T. His role was to make sure the Queen Mother's life and diary ran like Swiss clockwork, which wasn't always an easy task. Part of his duties, he explained to me one evening, involved not only organising her daily schedule but also making all her drinks, the preparation for which had involved months of doing little but learning how to mix spirits. It must have been a comedown to go from the Gulf War to mixing gin and Dubonnet—the Queen Mother's favourite tipple—but he took it like an officer and a gentleman. By having a few stiff ones himself. 'Drink?' was the first thing he'd say whenever I went to St James's. His office in Clarence House, where I often waited while he finished royal chores, contained very little furniture—an enormous desk, an odd-looking folding screen, a sofa and some personal photos of the Queen Mother—but it did have the most extraordinary drinks cupboard, offering everything you needed to pour The Royal Drink and more. It was so big you could have had a ball with all the leaders of state in there. I remember peering in it one day trying to find bottom-shelf liquor, but there was none. It was as if Berry Bros, the upmarket wine shop next door, used it as an additional cellar to stock all the good alcohol. There was so much premium liquor floating around the Queen Mother's household, it was like a posher version of *Ab Fab*. Only with a few more jewels.

I had to catch a few fleeting seconds with my boyfriend when I could because he was usually busy doing far more important things with far more important people—like prime ministers and presidents. Other times he would be frantically running chores for his gracious but understandably time-poor employer, who relied on him to do her day-to-day errands. One evening I turned up at Clarence House (by this time the sentry simply let me pass through the gate with a wave and the senior courtiers happily ushered me in the back door— something I always had terrible trouble adjusting to) only to find he was out buying Will and Harry Christmas presents on behalf of their beloved grandmother—who couldn't exactly pop up to Hamleys toy

CHANEL
PARIS

store on Regent Street for a spot of last-minute shopping. (He came back with water pistols—not a gift I would have chosen, but I'm sure they got a kick out of spraying the corgis on the back lawn.) I thought I had a difficult life but, next to his job, anything I did looked positively insignificant.

My new London life settled into an odd routine: tapping out features for magazines during the day; splashing from one cocktail glass to the other at the various work-related cocktail parties I was lucky enough to be invited to during the afternoon and evening (I was introduced to A.A. Gill, Frederick Forsythe, Clive James, Jan Morris and Bill Bryson among others, but I was usually so stressed about making it to St James's in time I barely remember what they said); and then dashing off to catch up with friends for a brief half-hour. In between all the tapping and the splashing and the dashing, I tore as fast as I could—usually in a black cab I couldn't afford—down to Clarence House. Naturally, the cockney drivers never believed me when I breathlessly gave the address.

'Clarence House?' they'd repeat in shock. 'What? *The* Clarence House?'

'Yes please,' I'd say politely, trying to redo my makeup in the darkness of the passenger cabin, change my shoes to a pair of less conspicuous heels and check that my cleavage wasn't too unladylike.

Eventually I kept a diary of the things I heard and saw, simply because even I started to find the events difficult to believe. One night I was invited into the palace's staff room to have a Christmas brandy with all the staff but I couldn't quite swallow the drink for the shock of seeing them all glued to *Home & Away* on TV. It was like going to the Vatican and discovering the Pope's personal staff watching *Oprah*. Another time my boyfriend told me how the Queen Mother would diplomatically brush off all those world leaders who wanted to see her by saying, 'Oh, I'm sure he's far too busy to come to tea with me!' before sneaking upstairs to watch reruns of *Fawlty Towers* and *Dad's Army*.

I heard about a rabbit warren of secret tunnels beneath St James's and Buckingham Palaces, which had entranced the Queen Mother since the war (a visitor to one of the palaces reportedly fell through a trapdoor in the floor many years ago and awoke from concussion to find the King bending over him with concern). I was told (although not in a detailed way) about the routine of daily life and evening dinners at Balmoral, where my equerry often had to go around the dinner table, shaking everyone awake. And I was enthralled by stories about the Queen Mother's fondness for men, which included her loyal and mostly homosexual staff. In fact, according to an article I once read in the *Observer*, the Queen Mother once said that, without them, 'we'd have to go self-service'.

The best stories I heard about the royals, however, were the ones that showed they were human. One of the courtiers told me a tale—which could have been just that—about the time President de Gaulle and his wife came to London on a state visit. Somebody—obviously trying to make polite conversation—asked Madame de Gaulle what it was that she was looking forward to most upon retirement. After a long pause she said: 'A penis.' There was instant silence and nobody dared breathe a word until the Queen, with her perfect French, replied: 'Ah, you mean *ha*-ppiness!'

Now really, how could you not be a royal lover on hearing a story like that?

In time, of course, it all ended. Most surreal dreams do at some point, and not just because reality and a royal family get in the way. The thrill of living London's high life faded after a while as my energy—and money—petered out. The expense of living such a life dulled the excitement of it, not to mention making it near impossible to carry off unless you were Her Majesty herself. Four months after arriving in London, in early 1995, I was ready to leave. The gloss had worn off. The glamour was gone.

The relationship break-up certainly contributed to the malaise.

It was difficult not to feel sadness when the phone calls plateaued out, even though I had known they would.

'Of course!' said my friend Holly, when I wept about it over a martini one evening. 'He's a cad. It's against their religion to have a girlfriend for too long. Cads need their amours to be perishable. Use-by date: one week after opening the top.'

Love, like many far-flung destinations, is rarely what we imagine it to be.

And so I fled to Paris. It was flashy, sublimely glamorous and full of an irrepressible confidence. Just what I needed after a demoralising romance. Besides, you know what they say: living well is the best revenge.

Then, as now, and indeed just as it was when I first set eyes on it for a few short days at the age of sixteen, Paris was lined with hope and edged with glamour. It was for those nostalgic for the aesthetic, the romantic and the quixotic. Those who wanted to be fabulous. Live fabulous lives.

I remember thinking, as I walked across the cobblestones one gorgeous night, trying not to blush at a wink from a cheeky waiter, that I felt strangely at home. For some reason, I finally felt, as the French say, happy in my own skin.

We live for certain moments in life. They're usually the moments when happiness falls unexpectedly around us and we realise that, for that brief second in time, we are extraordinarily content. These moments can be potent. They can make us believe that all moments can be like this, even though the reality is that they are as rare as that other ideal: The Perfect Life. They are so potent we will do anything to prolong them, hoping against hope that they will lead us into a kind of permanent beatitude.

My Paris sojourn didn't last long. Eventually, after a few weeks, I had to return to London: to the reality of journalism and deadlines and life. But I found it hard to forget that moment. And so now, in my thirties, after a punishing career in magazines, I have decided to return to my favourite city to see if I can recapture the magic of the place that first bewitched me at sixteen and then at twenty-four and for years thereafter. I want to see if I can rediscover the Paris I remember, and perhaps also find a little romance, if there is any to be found.

You see, the truth is, we all secretly want the fantasy. We want the martini-fuelled magic; the richness of a foreign romance. Even if it's only with a city we love.

And so I'd like to welcome you to my life, this Parisian life: one that has turned out to be far more fabulous than I could ever have imagined.

. 2 .

Desires and
Doisneau Moments

Paris, they say, is the city that changes least. After an
absence of twenty or thirty years, one still recognises it.

Marguerite Duras

Few places have been more soliloquised, anthologised and romanticised
by writers, artists, poets, journalists, publishers and people in floppy
hats drinking *pastis* than my favourite Parisian neighbourhood, the
sixième, or sixth, *arrondissement*. The *grande bourgeoisie* may prefer the
heavy elegance of the sixteenth and seventeenth arrondissements,
but it is the sixth where the magic really happens. One part myth,
one part fantasy and one part intellectual debate (and never more so
than now, when the luxury fashion brands threaten to smother the
area's bohemian character), the sixth is the Paris of our dreams. It is
so cherished, even by those haughtier souls on the Right Bank across
the river (who begrudgingly admit that it contains the soul and spirit
of *le vieux Paris*, the old Paris) that most Parisians couldn't imagine the
French capital without it.

I love this area. I always have. Even when I landed here, heartbroken and broke after my London affair. I love the endearing bohemia of it all; the fact that you can, while sipping a drink, still fall in love with a Sartre-obsessed *philosophe* sporting a black poloneck and a Catweazle beard. I love how, despite the 'boutiquification' of St-Germain, a gentrification lamented by the Left Bank traditionalists, you can still glimpse some of the old-time glamour and poetic spirit amid the new louche luxe. I love the fact that Hemingway and Fitzgerald and the rest of the American expats idled here on their way to fame and greatness, living on little more than the scent of drink and cigarettes. And how thousands of new Hemingways and Fitzgeralds experiencing the Paris rite of passage continue to polish the café chairs in their expensive jeans in the hope that some of the famous St-Germain inspiration will fall onto their Apple Mac laptops. I even adore the transparent elitism of it all—*le snobisme*, they call it—and the funny sniffiness of the area's cool tenants, a sophisticated mix of celebrities, gallery owners, artists (most of whom are filthy rich these days rather than just filthy) and book editors (the sixth is the heartland of Paris publishing). And I love the way the quarter never wavers in its pursuit of glamour and style. It is a place that always perfectly captures *l'air du temps*—the spirit of the times.

I have tried to like other parts of Paris: the historic first, the evocative fourth, even the lofty air of the sixteenth, but the affection and sentiment aren't there. The sixth, nestled quietly beside the river, is my spiritual home. The writer Henry Miller once remarked that 'to know Paris is to know a great deal', but to know the Left Bank, I think, is to know even more. If Rome is, as literary critic Anatole Broyard once put it, 'a poem pressed into service as a city' and New York an energised, explosive editorial bashed out with emphatic passion, then the Left Bank is very definitely a black and white film clip with a soulful jazz soundtrack. And you can't help but fall in love with the mystique and the romance of it all.

Interestingly, the fashion and travel sets have for years tried to pinpoint the city's 'new St-Germain', citing places like the funky Marais and the supremely cool Canal St-Martin districts north of the Seine as the new places to hang out, but truly stylish Parisians, including Karl Lagerfeld, Hubert de Givenchy, Marc Jacobs, Sonia Rykiel, Roman Polanski and Catherine Deneuve, stick steadfastly to this side of the Seine.

It's early autumn as I write this in my tiny apartment near the St-Sulpice church, and the season is settling comfortably over the Left Bank like a woollen scarf wrapped around the city's neck. Most people don't realise that Paris is more beautiful going into the colder months than at any other time. Under a dignified sky of Dior grey, you can see the 'bones' of the city, including its noble architecture, through the brittle branches of the trees. Somehow, the city seems finer, grander, more spectacular. The shimmering cognac shade of the Seine under the morning sun (which changes through the day to a luminous petrol blue and, finally, to a silver the colour of evening slippers at twilight), the grand grey of the famous cobblestone avenues and the fine oyster-shell grey of the buildings combine to give the city an almost gentlemanly feel. The city is distinguished, poised and more handsome than a Frenchman in black tie.

This morning, as I walked out into the place St-Sulpice, where the morning light was still blinking in bleary reluctance over the buildings, you could smell the new season in the air. In the Luxembourg Gardens the park was being re-dressed for autumn with a light coat of copper leaves, while over in the organic market at boulevard Raspail, plump pumpkins and squashes were replacing strawberries, cherries and lavender on the open-air stalls. The rain, which had fallen lightly like pearl-grey tulle through the night, had stopped, although the streetlamps still shone like Cartier diamonds in the pale light. And everywhere you looked, there was a compelling beauty that made the 'oh' catch in your throat. The city was, in all its autumnal splendour, a romantic pastiche of poetic gestures, and it was perfect. Just perfect. The kind of day that makes you believe the ideal can be real.

I am not the only one who feels this strange and all-consuming seduction. All over Paris, people—even the Parisians themselves—are rediscovering and remembering how beautiful and sensual their city can be. Call it a *dalliance française*, if you'll forgive the pun, but everyone's falling a little in love with Paris all over again.

The French have a phrase for it—*ça bouge*, which roughly translates as 'things are happening'. And indeed they are, thanks to *la Révolution*.

You see, several years ago, a group of famous creatives realised that their city was suffering from idleness and inertia and needed something of a makeover, if not a complete boot camp experience. Designers like Marc Jacobs, Hedi Slimane, Stella McCartney, Karl Lagerfeld and Phoebe Philo (then at Chloé), along with Thierry Costes, and even Claude Challe of the Buddha Bar noticed that Paris was pining; that it wasn't the Paris it used to be, and that *le désarroi français*—an overwhelming sense of helplessness and gloom—had gripped the city. And so they undid their elegant French cufflinks, rolled up their sleeves, and started injecting some new life into the place. Their aim was to make Paris the city of appearances—of glamour, of grandeur, of spectacle again.

Slowly, Parisians caught on to the feeling—*Parisitis*, they called it—and, infected by the new energy, rediscovered the famous frivolity and *joie de vivre* that had been missing for so many years. *Paris, le retour*, proclaimed the media at the return of the Parisian spirit. People began dressing up to go out again. And salsa dancing in the afternoons out at Belleville. And tangoing in an old train station on rue de Bagnolet until the early hours. While in places like Ménilmontant and rue

Oberkampf the bars were akin to jungles: you needed a machete to hack your way in. Gone was the Gallic depression and in its place was a feverish new excitement assisted by the non-stop musical beat known as 'French sound' (think of the Buddha Bar CDs). Suddenly, Paris was cool again.

Now, wherever you go in the world, you can't avoid the place. Everyone, everywhere, it seems, is moving towards the light as Paris once again shows off its charms. From LA to Copenhagen, people are talking about 'some hot new French designer' or 'some cool new Parisian club/CD/café/*quartier*'. Paris is aflutter with creativity. And the place is humming. Even New Yorkers, a group of fiercely patriotic urbanites who are famously loyal to their own little patch of Manhattan cement, have started drifting across the Atlantic to see what all the fuss is about. While it's not quite the kind of new post–World War II St-Germain-des-Prés that many sentimental hearts would adore, there is nevertheless a new and intoxicating spirit about the city. As Karl Lagerfeld wrote in the *International Herald Tribune*: 'And once again one has the feeling that the lights are turned on again in Paris …'

Even the polls reflect the new French spirit, with Parisians declaring themselves 'optimistic' for the first time a decade. And for the famously melancholic French, that's saying a lot.

Now that I'm here, I can't believe I ever considered being anywhere else. All my life I have imagined idling through these side streets, bewitched by these very scenes. It is almost as if all those writers and artists rubbing the café chairs and coffee cups and stairs have given the place a particular patina. According to Henry Miller, 'the streets sing, the stones talk. The houses drip history, glory and romance …'

Despite this overwhelming passion for the place, which many people feel—and not just the French—it has taken a long time to get to the point where I have the money, the time and, perhaps most importantly, the thirty-something motivation to make the idea of being in Paris a reality. I thought I might have drifted back here a little later in life, when I was wealthier or had met a Frenchman, or had simply become one of those eccentric, opinionated old travel writers who floats around the world and writes about foreign destinations in a mostly acerbic style with the kind of crankiness that comes from being sixty-five and discovering that nobody knows how to make a good G&T. But fate has a way of dragging you off the path you'd planned and forcing you to experience places, people and insights it thinks you might need at a particular point in time. Paris is my detour. It's a long way off the freeway I thought I would be on, especially after years of steadfastly focusing on a career path and moving from city to city to get where I thought I needed to be. But now that I'm here, I'm grateful. To use a well-worn cliché, I feel like I've come full circle.

The last ten years of my life have been quite complex. So complex, I wouldn't know where to begin unravelling them. They were mostly good years, and I feel fortunate for them, but they were also exigent at times. Challenging is an overused word, and more suited, I feel, to those with serious problems such as life-threatening illnesses, but they were certainly testing times.

When I returned to London that winter, after nursing my bruised heart in the cafés of Paris, I threw myself into work. Productivity is always the best remedy for dejection. When an old friend rang mid-March to invite me to the Oxford–Cambridge Boat Race on 1 April, I couldn't believe it was already spring. When the race came around, we cheered the two teams on then followed the throng to the West End to continue the celebratory drinking. There, in some overdecorated, Australian-themed pub, under a fake country fence and a worryingly unstable imitation of a dunny door hanging off its hinges, I met a handsome, six-foot, dark-haired scientist who bought me a drink. Six weeks later, he proposed.

We married at the Chelsea Registry Office, London's version of Las Vegas, only a lot more chic, and without the Elvis impersonators of course. We married again in Australia, for the benefit of those friends and family members who couldn't make it to the UK. By the time the second ceremony was over, I knew I'd married the wrong man. Twice.

It wasn't my dear husband's fault. I think part of me was still in love with the equerry. I'd also always dreamed I would meet someone in romantic circumstances, not underneath a fake dunny door, and that I would be proposed to in some idyllic spot—perhaps by a river after a picnic, or in some secluded place by the sea (Santorini, maybe)— and not in another rustic pub under more dodgy decorations. Again, this wasn't my husband's fault. I was touched that he even asked me. But I'm sure the casualness of everything added to the eventual disenchantment of it all.

And then there was the honeymoon, an overpriced jaunt to Tahiti where we were both so jetlagged and heat-struck we were incapable of movement let alone any kind of matrimonial consummation, and so spent the entire five days staring at the ceiling fan whirring around the five-hundred-dollar-a-night hut. I always thought I'd have a wonderful honeymoon, with lots of passionate sex and days spent doing nothing but debating the appropriate time to knock the top of the bubbly while calling each other 'wife' and 'husband' with glazed-eyed love. Instead, we barely spoke—Scott was furious at the prices of things, while I was despondent at the situation—and after a teary session in which I pleaded to go back to London, we packed up our fragile marriage and caught the plane home.

We lasted for four years, mostly because I didn't want to let Scott down. But the whole time I felt like I was dying inside. We eventually came back to Australia, where I finally summoned up the courage to call it a day. When Scott, in bewilderment, asked why, all I could reply was: 'I'm sorry, honey: it's too little, too late.' I needed intimacy. He needed a career. Like many couples, we had simply drifted apart.

Ironically, the split served to propel my previously languishing career into top gear, and I spent the next five years working my way up from a features writer to a columnist and then, finally, an editor, all the time longing for London and Paris. I was particularly nostalgic for the latter city, which I'd come to know from all my excursions, because I felt it represented the answer to all my romantic dreams. I naively believed everything good about the world stemmed from Paris and France. Apart from Tahiti, of course, but the French bombed that, so obviously they felt strongly about the overpricing too.

While I was steadfastly working, however, most of my friends began drifting away from corporate life. Unbeknown to me—probably because I was too preoccupied with kneecapping magazine deadlines and to-do lists to notice—they became infatuated with other things, such as pregnancies and mortgages, and raising cute toddlers in the suburbs. Suddenly children were the new handbags, and everyone I knew was giving up work in order to settle down and breed beautiful offspring. Babies, as one friend wittily put it, were the new black.

This wouldn't have been so bad but for the fact that, roughly around the same time, I found out I was infertile. Due to an innocuous urinary infection that occurred more than a decade earlier, my dreams of having a big family dissolved virtually overnight, leaving me not only with memories of an empty marriage, but a future as barren as a country paddock in drought.

Now I don't think these issues are really that significant in the scheme of things. People suffer much worse than divorce and infertility every day. And I'm grateful for knowing my husband. I still consider him a lovely man. But the pain of a childless future continues to make my eyes shimmer with tears at times, much to my dismay. And I have to be careful at Christmas that I don't get too despondent, especially around children—although this is usually fixed by taking my nieces out shopping and buying them half of the city until the credit card begins to convulse. Facing friends with swollen stomachs can also make me uncharacteristically shy, and when dinner party debates shift to c-sections and childcare, I usually find an excuse to clear the table. On top of The Baby Issue, there are other things to contend with in life, such as The Workload Issue, which many professionals, childless or not, are facing more and more in the modern-day workforce. With longer hours, heavier workloads and less time to do everything, many people, journalists and editors included, are facing a more challenging existence than ever before—and also a more competitive one. If you don't put in the time there are a thousand other would-be writers ready and waiting behind you to step in and do your job.

I think it's because of all these issues that I decided one night a few years ago, as I was leaving work at two in the morning for the third night in a row (midnight finishes had been a weekly occurrence for more than three years) and struggling to hold back tears of sheer exhaustion, there could only ever be one cure for my malaise. The place that had comforted me when I'd left London all those years ago. Paris.

I started formulating a new to-do list. If I could only visit Paris every now and then, I reasoned, it would be enough. But if I could find a way to extend these stays out until eventually, perhaps, they all rolled into each other, well, it would make up for not having the picket fence life and the perfect family I thought I would be blessed with by this age.

So, armed only with enough knowledge of the language to recognise Chanel, Christian Louboutin and Louis Vuitton, I made plans. Figuring I could make a small living from writing, not only magazine articles but also books on architecture, design and style, I pencilled out a strategy that involved maintaining a base in Australia, which enabled me to continuing editing—although I eventually crossed over from magazines to books, and full-time to freelance—and then slowly, slowly, establishing a life in Paris. A part-time life at first, but hopefully a full-time one before I turned too old to enjoy high heels.

So I packed up and went to Paris again, searching for the city of my youth and my dreams: the Paris that had rescued me all those years ago. I wanted a place that wasn't about social pressures, possessions and perfection but the small pleasures. The things that give us meaning and joy when others can't. The things that make life worthwhile.

Through a friend of a friend I found a tiny apartment on the Left Bank for a not-so-tiny price. I could also stay there virtually any time, when it wasn't let to tourists, since the owner had gone to New York to work. Here, in this new neighbourhood full of possibility and promise, I found Parisians who didn't ask when I was going to settle down and have a baby but directed me to the best *boulangerie* and gave me hints on cooking *coq au vin*. I found places—from secret gardens to quiet squares—that were so beautiful I wanted to dawdle an entire afternoon, soaking up the scene. And, through increasingly extended periods in Paris, I mapped out a new life: one that was as different to my Australian one as stilettos are to thongs.

I still consider myself a permanent resident of Australia, for that is where I mostly work, but my life is slowly drifting towards France with the same certainty that women drift towards shoe stores at sales times. I may still be an outsider in France but my heart will always belong to Paris. One day I will wake up here, look out the window, and simply refuse to leave.

Each day here is different, but they all revolve mostly around writing freelance articles for travel and lifestyle magazines, taking photos, sitting in quiet cafés, wandering picture-perfect streets, and remembering the sheer joy to be had in the magic of life in a foreign place. I have discovered an exquisite bistro where the tables are so small they could be upside-down exclamation marks, but the waiters don't care if you stay all day. I spend the afternoons strolling tiny alleyways little bigger than my hips, where, if I'm not careful, passing a broad-shouldered stranger can turn into a spontaneous love affair. I practise my French with my neighbourhood pharmacist and then repeat the same lessons with the lovely baker next door. I flirt with the cheesemaker and pick up style tips from the windows of Yves Saint Laurent. I don't mind that I don't have children or a career resembling that of my high-flying friends, because I have Paris. And that's enough for now.

It is not so much the city that I love, although that, too, is seductive in a way only Paris can be, but the people. Parisians are difficult to understand—even they admit that—but while they are maddeningly complicated they are also charming, suave (even my butcher has the smoothness of Cary Grant), and have more wit than Dorothy Parker, the Duchess of Windsor and Diana Vreeland combined.

Of course, the French have their faults. But don't we all? They can be irascible, formal, unfriendly, indifferent and utterly, annoyingly arrogant. But so can the English. The French just suffer more from the reputation. The London *Times* once printed an article that suggested many foreigners loved Paris but believed the biggest problem with the city was that the French lived there too. Damn the French, was the tone of the piece. Damn them for ruining a perfect good city. How dare they?

What the journalist failed to understand is that Paris *is* what it is because of the Parisians. Okay, so they have a penchant for posturing and are known for their uncompromising opinions on style, sex and what to put on a plate, but there is still a wonderfully generous spirit lurking beneath all that attitude. Let me give you an example …

The second time I came to Paris, in 1994, I was inconsolable, as the more dramatic French would say. When I landed here after my failed affair with the English equerry the first thing I did was smoke a cigarette, which made me sick, and the second thing I did was drink my weight in G&Ts, which made me even sicker. Once I had punished my body enough, I rang an Australian friend who lived in Paris to see if he wanted to come out and wallow in depression with me. 'Sure,' he said, because he was always up for a good time, and so

we dressed up and went out to lose ourselves—and our consciences—
on the Left Bank.

Unfortunately, Paris was in the midst of one of the city's famous
métro strikes at the time and not a lot was happening. Paris during
a strike is a little like trying to walk home after a couple of bottles
of very good wine: there's a lot of effort going on but you're not
necessarily getting anywhere. The French love to strike—they're
all little revolutionaries at heart—and even those who complain
about the inconvenience are quietly thrusting their clenched fists
in their air in patriotic support of their aggrieved countrymen. The
only ones it really bothers are the foreigners, and really, who cares
about them anyway?

So when my friend Rob and I set out on our anticipated crab-
crawl of the city's finest drinking establishments we found ourselves
unable to reach many of them because we needed a *métro* ticket to do
so. And there wasn't a working train around.

Undeterred, Rob stood out in the street—which was terrifying,
because we were on the Champs-Élysées at the time—and not so
much hailed a taxi as threatened, through a means of aggressive hand
signals and Tiananmen Square–style body tactics, to stop the first one
by brute force if it didn't pull up beside us.

Naturally the driver of the first car that hurtled along the Champs-
Élysées screeched to a furious halt in front of us and started screaming
French-accented abuse. I couldn't quite understand what he was
saying but it didn't sound as though he was too delighted to have come
across a couple of passengers on what was probably his way home to
a cold beer and a warm wife.

'*Bonjour,*' said Rob facetiously through the verbal gunfire when the
gentleman finally stopped for a breath, and then quietly opened the
door for me to slide into the back seat.

Shocked at our audacity, the driver continued to mouth a stream
of French words that, while difficult to translate in the heat of the

moment and the thick cigarette smoke of the interior, seemed to refer to someone's mother, and what kind of woman she was—not a very nice one, apparently. I also picked up a few phrases that, while I couldn't be sure, seemed to allude to what he would happily do to her that the rest of Paris hadn't done already.

Now I had never met Rob's mother but I don't think she would have recognised, let alone appreciated, half the sexual positions this Frenchman was describing. (I could tell they were something to do with sex from the way he gripped his wrists in front of him, angrily thrust his pelvis forward, and then stuck his middle finger up at us in the rear-vision mirror.)

Pleasantries exchanged, Rob sat back in his seat and calmly told the driver where to go. Which was somewhere on the Left Bank.

The Gallic taxi driver stared at him in a disbelieving manner. And then, obviously not having the slightest idea what to do with a clearly deranged man and a bewildered, slightly frightened girl sitting firmly in the back of his smelly car, he finally said something that resembled '*Baaaahhhhh*', and angrily put the car into Drive.

And that's when the real terror began.

The man tore with bad-tempered urgency at what felt like 120 kilometres an hour through the city, careening down lanes the size of newspaper columns into alleys barely bigger than a Diet Coke bottle, sliding around corners on two screeching wheels and lurching close to other taxis in an increasingly worrying fashion. We drove so close to one I swear I could smell what the other driver had eaten for lunch.

'*Tête de lard!*' raged the driver at his fellow drivers. '*Arrrhhghhggghhh.*'

In the back seat, Rob slunk back into the upholstery, gripping the door handle, which was slowly coming off in his hand, while I quietly clutched the window frame, which had fallen into my lap two minutes before.

I felt sick, and we hadn't even had a drink yet.

I think we circled the city five times that night. We ended up, by

✢
La Vie
Parisienne

some quirk of navigation, possibly because the driver was following the Deranged Taxi Driver's Map of Paris, circling the Arc de Triomphe on the place Charles-de-Gaulle, which vaguely resembles a merry-go-round, except that it's not very merry. We zigzagged around it in a sort of unhinged fashion until we finally veered near enough to one of the twelve exits, and then we flew off like a pinball.

When the driver finally screeched to a halt beside the St-Germain-des-Prés church, Rob staggered out and fell onto the pavement, still clutching part of the door. I would have joined him but for the fact that my face was stuck tight against the back of the front passenger seat since the driver had decided to brake suddenly at the sight of a hooker he knew.

Rob reached shakily into his wallet and paid the man, adding a generous tip as a kind of grateful thank you for allowing us to reach the Left Bank alive.

'*Non, non—gardez la monnaie!*' he urged the driver, telling him to keep the fistful of notes he threw nervously onto the front passenger seat.

I was still incapable of speech, let alone any kind of rapid movement, and so Rob grabbed my hand and helped me down the street in search of any stiff drink we could find. Even if it was only a bottle shop with a special on hard spirits.

The first bistro we plunged into was the kind of small, unpretentious place you don't think you'll ever remember again once you leave: a cheap *bar ordinaire*, as the Parisians call them. Barely the size of a napkin, it was thick with smoke and had a black sign with worn metallic lettering and metal tables that bore the patina of countless *rendezvous*. The zinc bar, which was barely wide enough for a wine glass, curved around and back to a mirrored wall, and rested on a solid and handsome but well-worn timber base that was scratched from decades of patrons hauling themselves up onto the rickety bar stools for a drink and a chat. Despite the faded interior, there was an aura of calm about the place. It invited you to linger, to see if there might actually be a memorable evening to be had here. Rob and I decided to stay.

The bistro, we were to discover, belonged to a man—a great strapping Frenchman with a face like Gérard Depardieu and a walk like Asterix—who introduced himself simply as Didier.

Now Didier could see straight off that we weren't in the mood to do a salsa and light a cigar. He could see immediately from my shaken, mournful, half-terrified expression that I wanted nothing more than Edith Piaf and a glass of something potent. So he ushered us respectfully into two chairs away from the rest of the patrons, told us not to worry about anything again that evening, and disappeared out the back to find something suitably intoxicating from the depths of his cellar reserve.

Rob and I looked at each other with shock. Was this the same city? Had we not just experienced the famous French nature in the back of the taxi?

'Perhaps the taxi driver took us to Copenhagen by mistake?' whispered Rob, a little perplexed by the unexpected generosity of this marvellous man.

After a few minutes Didier returned, puffing slightly from the journey down to his secret cellar, and held out a dusty bottle that looked like it had been hidden since the war. The first one. If not the Napoleonic one.

'This … this is something special,' he said, gazing lovingly at the label as if it was his first-born and ignoring the cloud of dust that swirled above our table. 'I will open this bottle for you. It will put the spirit back in your feet.'

Rob, who was always happy to put spirits anywhere in his body, sat back with renewed excitement, his taxi nightmare suddenly forgotten. You could see his eyes dance with anticipation. A wine from the war!

I tried to temper his enthusiasm. 'Somehow I don't think it will be a Château Mouton Rothschild, Rob,' I warned gently. But he wouldn't be calmed. Here he was, in Paris, in some atmospheric little bar on the Left Bank, having just survived a near-death experience with a murderous taxi driver, and now he was about to dine with a depressed, half-drunken girl who might, with any luck and a little more wine, become even more depressed and more drunk and want some serious comforting. On top of all this, he was about to imbibe a wine that hadn't been touched since, well, who knew when? Possibly since the American troops left the Moulin Rouge.

Didier, who had gone off to find a new bottle opener, perhaps one that was hardy enough to uncork this cellared treasure, returned, apologised for having been gone so long—'I have a very big cellar,' he said, as Rob's eyes grew wider—and proceeded to open the bottle.

As the three of us watched, the cork came out with a slow and promising *thwump!* Didier took a sniff. His eyes rolled. Rob leaned forward eagerly. Didier sniffed again.

'*Ah oui,*' said Didier, wrinkling his nose as though he had died and passed into some aromatic heaven. '*Oh ta ta!*' More onomatopoeic adjectives followed. Rob looked like he might wet his pants from the excitement, and he hadn't yet tasted a drop.

'Sniff,' urged Didier and Rob didn't need any further encouragement. He stuck his inelegant nose right in. I wasn't sure if I wanted any of this wine anymore, after all these snotty wet noses had been nuzzling the top of the bottle, and wondered if it would be impolite to ask for a glass of water.

'What do you smell, eh?' urged Didier.

Rob considered the aroma. And then shrugged, looking slightly deflated as if he had disappointed his new teacher with his ignorance.

'It is *la campagne,* the countryside!' said Didier. 'It is the Loire! Here—can you smell it?' He shoved the bottle under my nose. I took a tentative sniff. And to my utter surprise I realised he was right. I could smell forests and paths and fireplaces at twilight. Although some of it could also have been cellar dust.

'Ça commence bien, eh?' said Didier.

And then we were ready to get very, very drunk.

Of course, being Paris and also Didier's bistro, we couldn't drink without an accompanying dish of something. While it might have been respectful to the wine it wasn't Didier's way. So he ushered his chef off to find something suitably full-bodied and grand to help celebrate the opening of this very fine vintage, and elevate us out of depression and into that magnificent state of bliss that can only come with a full stomach, an even fuller bladder and slurred speech.

Later, I felt that it should have been called *dégustation* with a side dish of indigestion. I lost count of the number of calories that passed through our mouths that night. I felt like I'd swallowed a truck. Full of livestock. Which hadn't quite died. I could feel one of the carcasses press against my stomach. Beside me, Rob's face had gone from rapturous and ecstatic to pale, wan, and eventually puce. He eyed the cold stone floor as if he wanted to roll himself out on its welcoming hardness, close his eyes and gratefully embrace death.

'Ça va?' said Didier repeatedly, as dish after dish appeared from the kitchen of what must have been a most industrious chef.

Out they came: the dishes of Bresse chicken and Charolais beef and *barigoule* of vegetables. The slow-cooked this and the sautéed that. I don't know what we ate that night but I'm sure the chef went through the alphabet of French food, from *abats* (offal) and *anguille* (eel) to *tête de veau* (calf's head in jelly) and *tripoux* (mutton tripe).

Finally, feeling utterly queasy and quite intoxicated, I had to say with the best manners I could summon up: *'C'est tout, merci,* Didier. No more, please.'

If all this magnificent food wasn't enough to fix our depression, the wine—which turned out to be incredibly sweet and also quite on the nose—was so potent, we were both well gone by the second sip. While Didier rhapsodised about its aroma, I could no longer fathom whether the smell was of the countryside, or three-day-old roadkill on the *Périphérique* motorway ringing the city.

Didier continued to gush about body and bouquet and something called *puissance*. I needed to go have a *puissance* in the ladies' room. And then a long lie down.

More bottles followed from the cellar and more slurping of liquid, and by the time midnight rolled around, we had not only cured any depression but well and truly been initiated into the friendship circle of Didier Lacasse.

We staggered out of the bistro sometime after midnight, having paid a bill that we couldn't read, and didn't care to. I'm sure we looked like puppets from *The Thunderbirds*, lurching down the street. We finally made it to my hotel room, where we both rolled onto my ratty little single bed and fell mercilessly into a deep sleep, fully clothed. Sex was the furthest thing from Rob's mind. He was simply hoping he could make it to morning alive.

The next morning we awoke with a hangover that could have bombed a small French island in the Pacific. Rob said goodbye, thanking me for the best night of his life, even if there had been no sex involved—at least none that he could remember. I hugged him, thanked him in return for his generous hospitality, and then took a walk through my beloved Luxembourg Gardens for some peace and fresh air: the best antidote to a pressing Parisian hangover.

Halfway around the gravel paths, I realised with a jolt that I could barely remember the night before, let alone a love affair that had ended weeks earlier. In that moment, as the epiphany hit me, I silently thanked Didier for saving my sanity. The French are like that, you see. Just when you think they're cold and disagreeable, they sweep you off your feet with their charm and their bombastic Burgundies.

That was one of my first experiences with French hospitality. And the memory of it has never left me. I tried to find Didier the next time I went back to Paris, several years later, but he had gone, and nobody knew quite what had happened to him. Someone murmured, with a grimace, that they'd heard he had fallen headfirst down the stairs into his wine cellar, a bottle of Bordeaux in his hand, and had had to retire to the country to recover from his alcohol-induced injuries. Someone else argued that he'd simply gone back to his family house in the Loire to look after an ageing uncle. Whatever had happened, it was clear he had gone for good, and that a sad emptiness now pervaded his beautiful old bistro.

I didn't like to ask what had become of his extraordinary cellar, deep below the street. I simply thanked the waiters for their kindness and left, hoping that Didier's treasured wine collection continued to give patrons and staff the same hearty pleasure it gave us that night.

Years on, I have come to love Paris with the same passion that Didier felt for that dusty bottle of badly aged alcohol. Sure, the city, like the wine, has its faults. But who can possibly resist it when it quietly saves our souls?

. 3 .

Lines and Light

UNCOVERING THE CITY'S SECRETS
AND PLEASURES

To breathe Paris conserves the soul.

Victor Hugo

One afternoon, a couple of bored editors at some of the world's leading newspapers and news services were sifting lethargically through the media grapevine for stories when they stumbled across a little article from the publication *Le Journal du Dimanche*. It immediately tickled their editorial fancies. The story, which raced through the world's media faster than frog's legs through a Frenchman's mouth, detailed a peculiar ailment known as Paris Syndrome, which was affecting a number of foreigners (particularly Japanese) paying their first visit to the City of Light. Paris Syndrome occurred when the reality of Paris didn't quite meet the expectation. Although it was likened to Stendhal Syndrome, Paris Syndrome is actually the reverse. The former, named after the nineteenth-century French author, struck when Stendhal visited Florence for the first time and was rendered so faint by the beauty of the place he had to go and lie down to recover. A Stendhal Syndrome sufferer is in complete awe of a place: it is everything they imagined and more. Those who suffer Paris Syndrome, however, don't quite know what they're experiencing. But it certainly isn't Paris.

More than a dozen hypersensitive tourists a year require psychological treatment as a result of the condition, reported the papers, most of them travellers who had come to Paris expecting a city full of sophistication, *Amélie*-like characters, fine French food and lots of Louis Vuitton. Finding instead that some parts of the city were ruled by rude shopkeepers, disdainful taxi drivers and arrogant maître d's, their shock is so severe that many have had to be urgently repatriated. Fortunately, most of the sufferers improve considerably once they leave Paris, but some suffer terrible relapses, so the news agencies say. Some even develop psychoses. *Le Journal* reported that two women even claimed there was a plot against them while afflicted, while another man become convinced he was the French Sun King, Louis XIV, and yet another thought he was being attacked by microwaves. The papers didn't detail what eventually happened to the first two women, but I heard that one started to imagine she was a Louis Vuitton bag. The other girl tried to buy her. And then found out the bag was a fake.

I read this story a few days after arriving in Paris for a visit and almost immediately, like the good hypochondriacal, faux-French girl I was, I started to panic. I had also noticed things about the city that hadn't quite lived up to my expectations, not only now but on almost every one of my previous visits. The shoes weren't as affordable as I'd hoped, for a start, and the acres of vintage Chanel I had been promised from fashion blogs touting the place as a shopper's dream were nowhere to be seen. Furthermore, I mused, the food was a far cry from the food I thought the French ate, give or take a *pomme frite* or two, and also didn't seem to reward you with a very French figure. In fact, the French diet, which seemed to consist of a lot of 'white' foods, like *pommes frites*, baguettes and brioches, *millefeuilles, choux,* foie gras, camembert and bowls of vichyssoise, was not only horrifically calorific but always threatened to clog up my intestines whenever I arrived. Two days into every visit, I realised suddenly, I suffered the same problem that befalls many foreigners whenever they come here: that famous French ailment known as *la constipation*.

The last time I suffered this, after a particularly rich dish at Ladurée, I knew I had to seek help. So I went down to my local pharmacy, a quaint little place on the corner that plasters odd advertisements for equally odd ailments all over the window—just in case you're not embarrassed enough by your condition already—and summoned up the courage to go in. Eventually I ventured inside and attempted to explain my abdominal problem in faltering French to the weary-looking pharmacist without going into too much messy detail.

'*Excusez-moi,*' I stuttered, not yet comfortable about using the much-used Parisian phrase '*Je suis constipée*' and not really wishing to say the words out loud anyway in front of two svelte, well-dressed French women who were buying their Clarins Beauty Flash Balm. After an agonising pause, I finally pointed to my intestines and then made an aggrieved face, to suggest there was a problem down below.

Without so much as a glance of concern, the pharmacist gave me a *tisane*—a herbal tea—with the rather dubious name of *pissenlit*, which seemed to be, from the weedy looking photo on the packet, a laxative distilled from dried-up old dandelions.

'Take this,' he said unenthusiastically, as if he dispensed the weedy tea every day.

Unfortunately, he said it so fast I couldn't quite comprehend the instructions, and thought—or imagined—that he went on to say, 'Take it *ten* times a day', rather than three. The only thing I could think was that the weedy tea was perhaps rather weak, and that you needed a lot of it to flush all the French food away.

I went home that night and studied the packet. And then, not understanding a word of it, finally decided to Google 'pissenlit' on the internet. It wasn't a rewarding search. What I found, on some obscure pharmacy site, was that 'pissenlit' actually meant to 'urinate in bed'. That didn't sound very appealing. Nor very ladylike, should I happen to meet a lovely French man the following night—especially one who slept on 1000-thread-count sheets.

Five hours and several *pissenlits* later, I had become more familiar with my bathroom walls than I perhaps would have liked. I was also beginning to feel that *pissenlit* should have perhaps been called *pissenlot*. Or simply, Partake-in-Toilet-Activities-So-Much-You'll-Consider-Never-Eating-French-Food-Again. I could feel my fantasies of an *Amélie*-style romance among the cobblestones of the Left Bank rapidly receding behind the reassuringly high pile of white French toilet paper.

As well as the absence of affordable vintage Chanel, cheap shoes and healthy salad leaves, I also couldn't fathom what had become of the romance in Paris: the famous *amour* that had been promised as part of any Parisian visit. This had obviously been an urban myth too, because nearly all the stores I walked into every time I came here were stocked with sex toys and other things that promised not so much romance but more of *un good time*. Even Sonia Rykiel, the stylish French designer who dresses most of the newsreaders on French TV, had allowed her daughter and artistic director Nathalie to stock the shelves with vibrators as well as shoes. (Although, admittedly, they looked discreetly like lipstick tubes, in case you wanted to hide one in your clutch purse.) I walked into Rykiel's Left Bank store to browse for a suit one day and left in a hurry, thinking I had somehow stumbled into a Pigalle porn store by mistake.

In fact, I think the absence of ready romance on tap was perhaps the most disappointing thing of all about Paris when I first came here, and the one thing that made me feel as though I suffered my own small form of Paris Syndrome. You see, when I was growing up, I half imagined that Paris was going to be bursting to the boulevards with gorgeous men, every one of them (or at least every third one) ready to offer a kiss, a wink and a seat by his side on the *terrasse* of an atmospheric Left Bank café, where they would pour a decent wine and proffer their undying love. I can't imagine where I got this idea. But the shock of the reality was certainly almost enough to turn me to Louis Vuitton. Not *into* Louis Vuitton as such, like the poor deranged Japanese woman. But certainly into the store, to seriously consider buying a handbag as therapy.

I think I imagined this because, as a gullible young university student, I saw a movie called *Henry and June*, a film that has now passed into that cult collection of French movies that includes *Betty Blue* and *Belle de Jour*. As with every other university student in the cinema and indeed the world, this film resonated long after the credits had rolled off the screen. Based on the diaries of the French writer Anaïs Nin, who met the American writer Henry Miller and his wife June in Paris in the 1930s and subsequently had affairs with both of them, the film was alternately thrilling and shocking. I can't remember much about the plot, although I know it had Uma Thurman in it somewhere, but I do remember that there were a startling number of tantalisingly erotic scenes in it: scenes showing couples writhing and sighing in dim doorways and shadowy alleys all over the city.

It made you imagine that this is what went on in Paris: naughty fondling in darkened doorways with people you shouldn't be doing naughty fondling in darkened doorways with—a sort of *liaisons dangereuses* for the modern age. I wanted to go to France immediately. I wanted to shed my prudish inhibitions and discover lust and longing in the stairways of the Left Bank. I wanted to forget my studies and fling myself with wild abandon into the arms of some inappropriate, ravishingly good-looking man called Philippe or François, and then finish by singing *'Non, je ne regrette rien'*.

It never happened, of course. But it didn't stop me coming to Paris, in the faint hope that one fine day, some day in the future, my titillating French Romance might still occur.

Thankfully, I am not the only one who has suffered a disenchantment of sorts when it comes to Paris, or indeed who has fallen for the urban myths and stories about the place in the first instance. Thousands of foreigners, men as well as women, have travelled to Paris over the years in search of hope, dreams and a new life of French fantasies. And it's fair to say that a large percentage of them have been influenced by Mr Henry Miller, and all the things he celebrated with gusto—namely, sex, drinking, beauty and all the rest of the vices that come with an empty afternoon, a full glass and an attractive drinking partner. In fact, for all his faults, Miller has to be credited for turning Paris into something of a cult destination, especially for travellers searching for Meaning and Love, rather than the less attractive Being and Nothingness promised by Sartre. Some people arrive in Paris armed with a *Lonely Planet* guide. The rest of us arrive with memories of *Henry and June* to guide us.

For those not familiar with Henry Miller—and you could be forgiven, because he's often overlooked in all the adoration showered on his compatriot Ernest Hemingway—the rakish, dashing writer and author of many books (most of them banned for their saucy content) is to Paris what David Beckham is to football. A marketing tool *par excellence.* While Hemingway and all the rest of the expats—including Miller's good mate Orwell—wrote about living on the edge of poverty amid the glamour and *pastis* of Paris, Miller wrote about living on the edge of a bed. Actually, make that many beds, since he hopped in and out of so many Parisian *boudoirs* there are those who believe he slept with half the city. He portrayed a sexier side of Paris with stories that took the city and made it alluring. And, not surprisingly, a lot more appealing. After Miller, foreigners no longer wanted to be a depressed dishwasher like poor George Orwell. They wanted to be Henry, living the high life. Well, who wants to be a dishwasher when there are far more attractive parts of the city to explore—like the parts of naked Parisians, for example?

Like all the great charmers of the twenty-first century—Hemingway, Bogart, Dean Martin, Frank Sinatra—Miller had something that made him irresistible. He not only knew women, he knew Paris—its personality and its most private parts. In fact, he knew the city almost as intimately as he knew his lovers. He felt his way through the streets like a blind man, caressing each scene, and memorising each perspective in order to immortalise it in print. He was as in love with Paris as he was with Parisians, and Paris—and Parisians—loved him in return.

Strangely, Miller discovered Paris quite late in his career. But that didn't stop him from embracing it, and its women, with open arms and an even more open mind. When he landed in the city, dressed to the nines (his father was a tailor), he immediately adopted an F. Scott Fitzgerald approach to the place. Paris was there to be consumed; to be celebrated; to be eaten; to be f—d. (Although Miller would have put all this in an even more indelicate way.)

After a few years of uninterrupted sex and the kind of pleasure that comes from being permanently drunk in Paris, he wrote a novel about it (as all writers try to do) entitled *Tropic of Cancer*, which was full of his favourite two things: f—ing and drinking (if you'll excuse my French).

It was so explicit, the United States censors immediately banned it on grounds of obscenity—which of course made every student from the Sorbonne to the American Ivy Leagues seek out coverless copies to sneak back home under their French-style trench coats. Almost overnight, Miller became a cult figure: a folk hero for that generation, and for every generation thereafter.

Funnily enough, I have never actually read an entire copy of this now-famous memoir. I've read other works by Miller but I think I've always been too embarrassed to buy *Tropic of Cancer*. It's difficult enough hiding the copy of *Juliette* by the Marquis de Sade whenever well-dressed guests come over for dinner. But now that I'm here in Paris, I think I should search it out. I have a feeling it will show the city in a whole new light.

This thought has prompted me to start a list of things to do in Paris, which I've prosaically entitled 'Things To Do In Paris'. I've created this list because I believe—or I quietly hope—that it will help with The Getting of (Parisian) Wisdom, which is something I aspire to whenever I come here. Most people come to Paris to climb the Eiffel Tower, wander around the Left Bank, fall in love, find themselves, lose themselves, or just be someone *other* than themselves for a little while. I come to Paris to do all this but also to try to be a better person—a wiser, kinder, more sensitive, less stressed, and generally more peaceful person. With a lot more style. Like Audrey Hepburn. Only without the gorgeous face and body, obviously.

The first thing I've pencilled on this list of Things To Do, after checking out Chanel, naturally, is 'Uncover the secret side of Paris', by which I mean the side better known to writers like Henry Miller and Ernest Hemingway. By following in the steps of these esteemed expats, particularly Miller (whom I admit to having a little crush on), I figure that I will find The Real Paris, not the Paris of guidebooks and internet blogs and syndicated newspaper stories. I will find the Paris that only truly dedicated devotees of the city bother to look for, and in

doing so, I surmise—or at least I hope with all my heart—that I shall
become just that tiny bit more Parisian.

I decide to start where all good Parisian students start: Paris's answer
to everything. No, not Monsieur Miller, but another much-loved icon:
the bookshop known as La Hune.

Located in the heart of the writers' and publishers' district near
St-Germain-des-Prés, near those other iconic haunts Les Deux Magots
café and the Café de Flore, La Hune is part of the literary history of the
quartier. For years it has been the favourite haunt of writers, publishers,
editors and anyone with a love of the written word, including all those
Left Bank *intellos* who loiter here late into the evening looking up
Balzac. There are many who feel that the Left Bank wouldn't be the
Left Bank without La Hune.

Perhaps the best thing about the store, apart from its fantastic
range, is that it has steadfastly refused to sell out to an international
conglomerate. This, of course, has only made its followers love it
even more. People flock here to soak up the history as much as the
atmosphere and the offerings. It is, quite simply, a Mecca for those
who love books and learning.

The store was renovated in 1992 and now has a slick, modern
feel, but there is still something about climbing the stairs to the
mezzanine level, where tables groan with architecture and art titles,
that fills book lovers, including myself, with a quiet thrill. It is a space
for contemplation, exploration and education. I've lost track of the
number of times I've come here for a browse and left with a pile of
tomes. You just never know what you'll find at La Hune.

It is early morning when I venture into the store, ostensibly to find
more sophisticated guidebooks on Paris than those I have brought with

me but also to search out a copy of Henry Miller's *Tropic of Cancer*.

I want to go early because it's unlikely there will be many people in the store then and I'll be able to source my book in peace. I don't want anyone to think I'm some kind of dirty girl searching for a book about sex. Some handsome, hip Frenchman, for example, who might be loitering in the philosophy section reading Alain de Botton.

Despite the hour and the absence of browsers, I can't help but feel as though I'm in the men's section of a newsagent, flicking furtively through a dirty magazine. I decide I need help to uncover the title and uncover it fast, so I can escape the store and go read it under the anonymous cover of an awning in a quiet café.

'*Excusez-moi, monsieur*, do you have any books by Henry Miller?' I ask the young guy restocking books, not knowing if he speaks English but hoping he will understand the famous name.

'Miller? Mmm ...?' He looks puzzled. 'Miller, Miller ... Ah! *Death of a Salesman*,' he says finally with a bright smile.

'*Er, non*,' I correct him, feeling myself blush from the cleavage up. '*Henry* Miller. Not *Arthur*. *Henry*.'

He is very perplexed, and I am at a loss as to how to explain the difference. I decide to try another tack. '*Henry et June?*' I say hopefully.

'Aaahh,' he says, with a clearly perceptible shift in vocal tone. And then, with what I think is a second sideways glance at me, shuffles off to find the 'other' Miller. The less respected one.

Five minutes later, I am exiting La Hune with a discreet bag under my arm, feeling more and more like I have just bought some porn.

I retreat to Henry Miller's favourite haunt, the Café de la Mairie on place St-Sulpice, where, over a fortifying Ricard, I spend the next few hours alternately staring out at the glorious square and its splendid parade of Parisians and reading the first few chapters of *Tropic of Cancer*. It is so explicit I wonder if I should put it down and purchase a *Vogue* magazine to hide it behind. The waiter winks at me knowingly when he brings me another glass and I contemplate whether to go home and read the book behind tightly closed shutters instead.

'Is everything all right, madame?' he says in English, setting down the drink.

'Yes, thank you,' I smile weakly, hiding the book between my knees.

I look across the square at the famous church. Henry wrote about the 'fat belfries of St-Sulpice' in *Tropic of Cancer* and, in the smoke swirling from the tables on the terrasse, I sense his ghost resting nearby, perched with a notepad in one of the chairs. He loved this café, and would often stop to write here undisturbed, looking up now and then to consider the world. The square hasn't changed much since those days and I think Miller, if he were here, would be happy to see it. Here, at least, his Paris—the Paris he loved—is still very much in existence.

Part of me wishes forlornly that I lived back then in the heady thirties, and that I knew Henry. In my eyes he is the perfect man. He was arrogant, certainly, but he was also filled with an infectious enthusiasm for life, love and women. He reportedly had a great sense of humour, as well as a great wit, both of which made him almost irresistible to the opposite sex. Erica Jong once described him as 'full of beans and braggadocio, overflowing with the lust to live and write'. You get the feeling she was a little in love with him too.

And then there was his voice: a captivatingly melodic and rich tone once described in *The Paris Review* as 'mellow, [and] resonant, but quiet bass with great range and variety of modulation'. It was a voice that competed with Humphrey Bogart's for sheer sex appeal.

But perhaps Miller's most endearing trait was his attitude. He eschewed possessions, which he felt could be falsely satisfying, and instead focused his attention on people and relationships. Ironically, he stumbled on this philosophy almost accidentally, and quite late in his life as well. He had come to Paris, like so many other writers and wanderers, searching for life and meaning, having broken up with June. He arrived with only a raincoat, a toothbrush, a razor, a notebook and a pen, and a wallet containing just ten dollars. But instead of being depressed about his minimal possessions and newly empty life, Miller discovered that the act of stripping back his material comforts was, in fact, cathartic, and resulted in making him more aware of the world. It also made him, in an odd way, into a much better writer. Fine clothes and a fancy career simply weren't important, he realised. Relationships, on the other hand, were.

I wish my ex-husband and I had learned such lessons earlier in our lives.

Leaving the café with the novel stuffed down the bottom of my bag, I walk south and eventually find my way to rue de la Tombe-Issoire, and then to Villa Seurat, a tiny, dead-end street held together with old cobblestones and atmosphere and heavy with the ghosts of Henry and Co.

It was here, to a top-floor studio at number 18, that Miller supposedly moved on the very day that *Tropic of Cancer* was published in September 1934, and remained until 1939. He later wrote that his happiest moments in Paris were those in the Villa Seurat. This tiny, private cul-de-sac symbolised, for him at least, the richness and spirit of Paris. 'The process of losing myself began at the Villa Seurat,' he would later recall.

I look up to number 18 to see if I can glimpse Henry's ghost, but all is quiet. For a brief moment I imagine I can hear the sighs of Anaïs Nin drifting out into the sunshine, but then the sound is gone and the street is silent again.

I want to raise a glass to The Great Man in a toast to him and his endearingly audacious ways. But I only have bottled water in my handbag, and I don't think Henry would approve.

Joseph Campbell,* a New York philosopher who knew a thing or three about the art of contemplation, once said: 'we're so engaged in doing things to achieve purposes of outer value that we forget the inner value ... the rapture that is associated with being alive is what it is all about.' Henry Miller himself echoed Campbell's reflections when he said: 'If there is to be any peace it will come through being, not having.'

At the risk of over-philosophising, I wonder how many people know this, or will even learn it in this increasingly rampant consumerist society? I know it has taken me many years to understand that a Louis Vuitton suitcase, a pair of Chanel shoes, an Armani suit and a Valentino dress will not make me happy, even if I *could* afford them. And a great career, a cute apartment full of faux-French pieces and a nice car will only go so far towards fulfilment as well.

What makes me happy, I've realised, is this: wandering through the quiet streets of Paris on a brilliantly sunny day, snacking on a bread roll bought from a beautiful little bakery and picking off the almonds to eat along the way.

I walk all the way back to the quiet beauty of the place St-Sulpice, and then onto the side streets near St-Germain-des-Prés and those *rues* that I have come to love: rue Férou, which is like a perfect laneway from a sleepy village in Provence; rue Jacob with its stylish design stores; and rue de Furstemberg, where the square is picture-perfect Paris. I walk slowly because then I can see the streets, the people, the shopfronts and ornate balconies, and the signs, which offer a typographical beauty that is unexpectedly rewarding for someone who has lived her working life on a diet of fonts and headlines. One of these signs—made up of an elegant white serif script swirled deliciously over a glossy black background so polished you could do your lipstick in its reflection—is so arresting, I have to stop and take a photo. It is,

* Both Miller and Joseph Campbell are, not surprisingly, revered in this city, where the art and beauty of simplicity is echoed in Parisians' daily rituals. Although Miller is perhaps adored more by those foreign students who come to Paris in search of cheap wine and memorable sex, while Campbell is appreciated by the French philosophers who spend their nights in search of memorable wine and cheap sex.

in all its monochromatic simplicity, quintessentially Parisian.

It is these things, I think as I stroll along with my bread roll, that really make up the fabric of Paris—the signs; the façades and architecture; the quiet streets and their gently wonky cobblestones; the wrought-iron balustrades and old wooden doors. These are the things that give Paris beauty and detail. If a magazine is identified by its masthead then Paris is identified by its icons and signs. In a way, they lead you around the city, drawing you into its corners. Who hasn't been seduced by the sexy swirl of a jazz club sign, beckoning you inside? Or a chocolate maker's window, promising rich pickings within?

Parisians have a phrase to describe such things, the little things they love most about living in their city. This phrase is *petits trésors*, which literally means 'the small treasures' of life. It refers to the captivating signs and tucked-away stores, the fabulous open-air street markets, the beautiful bridges and serene backstreets, and the utterly unforgettable cul-de-sacs you discover and never want to leave. Most people discover their own *petits trésors* after a period of time in Paris. Everyone owns some shamelessly sentimental Paris moment, even if it's just the first time they caught a view of the Eiffel Tower from the back of a Parisian taxi.

I walk back down my favourite side streets and alleyways, discovering sunny corners in which to lose myself for the afternoon. I love the fact that the city allows you to walk. And, as you're walking, to think, consider and contemplate. When the body is going at three miles an hour, the senses are allowed to relax and embrace the subtleties of the city: the gentle shades of the architecture (my favourites are the church-white façades with the Chanel-black doors), the sounds of the streets (conversations, arguments, arias drifting out of windows) and the rich scents. If I close my eyes I can always smell something in Paris: heady Guerlain cologne, delicious offerings from busy patisseries, big bunches of white lilies at picturesque flower stalls, and rich coffee beans being ground for the day ahead.

Walking also allows you to experience parts of Paris you simply wouldn't see if you were underground or in the back of a taxi, such as the hundreds of waiters rushing around serving *ballons* of Beaujolais; the *grandes dames* in their Chanel discussing life and grandchildren in the windows of the city's *salons de thé*; the sheer theatre and spectacle of it all. It allows you to *engage* with the city. You do not need to worry about Paris Syndrome when you're taking a stroll through the city.

One day I was out wandering the streets near St-Germain when a restaurateur I saw on my daily reverie suddenly stopped sweeping the *terrasse* in front of his bistro and raised his head to give me a smile.

'*Bonjour madame!* Out walking again?'

'*Oui, monsieur*,' I said pleasantly, thrilled that a real Parisian had not only recognised me but had also taken the time to stop and chat. I stopped and smiled broadly at him.

'*Un petit verre?*' he said unexpectedly, offering me a glass.

'*Merci, oui*,' I said excitedly in very bad French, raising my eyes in surprise.

He grinned and indicated for me to take a chair on the *terrasse*. So I sat down, feeling sublimely grateful, and not just because my new French shoes were killing me. He returned with a bottle of red, filled a glass, and then gestured to the chair beside me, asking if it was okay for him to sit down.

'Of course,' I replied, and so he joined me for a drink.

His name was Saul, he said, and he had seen me walking past many times. He was curious to know what I did. Was I a professional *flâneur*?

'*Oui*,' I said slowly, because, although I was watching his mouth and his gestures closely, I really couldn't understand a word he was saying. (I only assumed he said this because I recognised the word *flâneur*, which means someone who likes to stroll.)

'Ah,' he replied, realising that I certainly couldn't understand a word he was saying and that I was merely trying to be conversational. And so he simply raised his glass with a grin. '*À la vôtre!*' he said, beaming.

'*À la vôtre*,' I grinned back.

And so we drank to Paris. It was the greatest chat I've never had.

The best thing about walking through Paris, apart from the aesthetic gifts and unexpected relationships it gives you, is that it's marvellously therapeutic for sorting through the flotsam and jetsam of day-to-day detritus. It's the best way to understand not only the city but also any issues that may be bothering you, no matter how big or small. I've worked through many a concern on a stroll through Paris's streetscapes, from the ghosts of babies I'll never have to the regret of a bad marriage that perhaps wasn't so bad after all but just not for me, and come out feeling content at the end. It is here you can take memory by the hand and, before you've strolled a little way, feel the regrets fall away. I've even considered business plans and mulled over commercial ventures pitched to me from friends back home while licking a lemon sorbet on the steps outside Berthillon ice-cream shop under a Fragonard sky. I've been inspired to write certain books standing on the Pont des Arts, staring down at the Seine. And I've set out my new life with hope and dreams while the warm breeze rustles the trees and *bateaux mouches* drift down the river, with a bloated accordion playing old French tunes from behind. Any kind of preoccupation can be considered, resolved and then packed away in a simple afternoon of idling around Paris. It's the best way to find order in the urban chaos of life; the best way to find perspective and clarity.

With the afternoon light fading, I set out for the tranquil calm of the Luxembourg Gardens. I want to visit one of my favourite Parisian cafés before the day draws to an end—an enchanting olive-green Hansel and Gretel-style hideaway of a place that's set magically underneath the trees in a corner of the park. It's not quirky by any means but it has a curious storybook feeling about it. You almost expect the woodcutter to emerge and doff his hat to you as he passes.

I take a seat under the shade of the trees, set down my handbag, camera and laptop, order a lemon drink with lots of ice, and feel the breeze refresh my spirit as I take in the parade of people through the park at this most beautiful time of day.

The air is still and warm and there is a kind of sensuality about the pale evening light that makes you believe there could indeed be something ineffably romantic about this city. People say that autumn is bittersweet and melancholic—the passing of another year into winter—but I think the season is more about new beginnings. It's about change, possibility, promise.

I think of all those who have been here in the gardens before me, drawing inspiration from its formal contours and playful spirit. Delacroix. Baudelaire. Chopin. George Sand. And Balzac, who apparently wandered around in a dressing gown, carrying a chandelier. (I don't believe this is actually true, but the image tickles me pink just the same.)

As I sit and smile at the thought of Balzac, a black-clad Frenchman sitting in a chair nearby clears his throat.

'*Bonjour, madame,*' he says politely.

'*Bonjour, monsieur,*' I reply bravely.

'*Travaillez-vous?* Are you working?' He nods at my laptop and the copy of *Tropic of Cancer* that rests beside it on the table.

'*Oui,*' I respond, not quite knowing how to explain what I'm doing with a copy of *Tropic.*

'Are you a writer?' he says in English, obviously noting my atrocious accent.

'Yes,' I say. '*Une journaliste.*'

At the mention of the word *journaliste*, he looks alarmed suddenly. It isn't the effect I had hoped for. I might as well have said that I was a high-class hooker.

'Ah,' he says awkwardly, as if to suggest it is the clichéd response of just about every blow-in who lands in Paris and orders a glass of spirits.

No really, I am, I want to plead, adding that it has been how I have made my living for fifteen years.

'I am *une professionnelle*,' I insist, accidentally using the slang term for a whore. He distances himself even more.

'Look—here is my business card!' I say, fumbling in my bag for the stack of cards that I always keep on hand. But he only looks more anxious and starts to edge slowly away from the entire conversation. As I rummage in my bag he grabs his coffee cup and newspaper and moves furtively to another chair.

As a warm rain starts to fall lightly on the city, I pack up my laptop and leave the park, taking a last look at the octagonal pond, which is now flecked with the first of the autumn leaves and the thick splatters of raindrops. I wander out onto rue de Vaugirard and take a last stroll. In the streets behind St-Sulpice, the florists are already doing chic little arrangements in the colours of autumn, their huge tubs of white roses now joined by elegant bundles of black twigs, orange lilies and ripe fruit, including plump pumpkins and pretty brown pears. There is a distinctly villagey feel about the area—the Odéon *quartier* is like France condensed in a perfect Parisian neighbourhood—and I smile at the sights that are charmingly clichéd: the open-air grocer with his baskets of asparagus kissing his wife as she restocks the potatoes; the butcher flirting with a regular customer as he packages up her quail for dinner.

I have read shelves and shelves of books about Paris, from Ernest Hemingway and Henry Miller to Diana Vreeland and George Orwell. But perhaps the best line I've ever read about the city was written by John Baxter, a writer, film critic and biographer, in his book *We'll Always Have Paris: Sex and Love in the City of Light*: 'all Paris stories are to some extent stories of love—love requited or unrequited; knowing or innocent; spiritual; intellectual; carnal, or doomed ...' More than anything I think this line encapsulates the city. Miller knew it; Ernest knew it; Anaïs knew it. Paris is a city full of possibility and promise, whether you come to forget a love affair, or lose yourself in a tantalising new one.

I wander home down rue Guisarde and sigh with happiness as I reach the door of my tiny studio. I light a white candle and look out into the night as the tiny spiral of smoke drifts out the window. High up in the night sky, past my neighbours' window and the silhouette of them making love, I can see the Parisian sky, which now stretches like dark denim across the city. All around me in the city people are kissing passionately; pouring wine; watching the last news broadcast of the day; thinking of their mistresses; making out in doorways. Paris is about to say goodnight.

I fall into my bed, blissfully content, listening to the neighbours practising their horizontal two-step. The disillusioned Japanese tourists may be happy to be repatriated, but I'm not ready to leave just yet.

. 4 .

All Bar Vin

FOLLOWING IN HEMINGWAY'S FOOTSTEPS

Paris, Paris. There is something silken and elegant about
that word, something carefree, something made for a
dance, something brilliant and festive, like Champagne ...

Nina Berberova

My rented Parisian apartment is tiny. Actually it is smaller than that.
To use the word 'tiny' is overdoing it. A 'tiny' apartment would be
luxurious compared to the size of my studio. It's an embarrassed
cough, really. A splutter of an apartment. When the agent first
showed me around the place, he sort of harrumphed awkwardly and
coughed, 'Voilà alors. Here it is,' as he pushed into the room. I followed
him eagerly, keen to see this chic little domain, which I had imagined
would look like something from a spread in *Elle Décor*. Unfortunately,
it didn't look anything like a spread in *Elle Décor*. Not even remotely.
It was, however, about the size of the two pages a spread in *Elle Décor*
is printed on. Give or take a centimetre or two.

Because of the narrowness of the apartment, we found ourselves, the little French agent and I, wedged awkwardly together between the galley kitchen and the bed. With our faces together. Like a couple of strangers in a nightclub on New Year's Eve.

'*C'est bon, eh?*' he smiled clumsily, as a plume of garlic breath erupted from his Gauloise-stained teeth. He then gave a little Gallic shrug, as if to say: 'Well, what do you expect for less than €200 a night, hey?'

I was at a loss for what to say—and not just because I couldn't speak much French.

I originally found this apartment through a friend of a friend who, upon hearing that I was desperate for accommodation in Paris, suggested airily that she 'might know someone who knows someone who might have a place to stay'. It's the age-old travel phrase that hints at many dangers. When you hear this you know immediately that it's not going to be a suite at the Ritz. You just hope it's not going to be a room at a homeless men's boarding house.

But when I arrived at the building, on a tiny cobblestone laneway behind St-Sulpice, it held all the promise of The Perfect Parisian Abode. There were jazz clubs right outside; an English-language bookshop around the corner; the Luxembourg Gardens on my doorstep; and even Catherine Deneuve as a neighbour. The only trouble was, like many Parisian apartments, it was situated on the top floor, up eight flights of rickety old stairs, with no working lift in sight. So we started traipsing up the stairs, the portly little Frenchman and I, but by the fourth floor I could barely stand up and the Frenchman, who looked like he'd never lifted more than a cigarette in his life, had turned white from lack of oxygen. When we finally pitched into the apartment and then became jammed between the sink and the bed, the stop for a rest was almost a relief.

Eventually his wheezing and gasping slowed, and with a theatrical sweep of his arm he pointed out the view (straight into the neighbour's bedroom), the bed, the bathroom, and the innovative kitchen-in-a-cupboard.

'*C'est magnifique, eh?*' he said, beaming.

You had to admire his technique.

Being the dutiful agent he was, he agreed that there were things about the space that weren't, well, quite like the Ritz.

'*La serrure est cassée,*' he admitted apologetically, nodding his head at the broken lock on the door, '*et ça ne marche pas,*' he added, waving at the useless kettle.

I must have looked stricken at these bits of information, especially the damaged lock on the door, because he tut-tutted and gave a little reassuring smile. 'It is fine; I fix!' he said in broken English. '*Peut-être,*' he added, bobbing his head hopefully from side to side with a doubtful expression in his eyes.

As if to show just how *magnifique* the apartment really was, he extricated himself from the space between the kitchen and the bed and went over to open the window. Which refused to budge.

Finally, he conceded that it was painted shut. '*Ça ne marche pas,*' he shrugged. '*Er, il y a un défaut,*' he explained, confessing that it had a little flaw.

'Do you think you could fix it?' I pleaded.

'*Peut-être,*' he sighed again, looking around the studio with an expression that seemed to suggest he was starting to feel grateful he didn't have to live here, with all these broken things.

There was a long pause as we both considered what to do. And then he brightened and looked at me, with what I imagined was supposed to be a smile under the haunting half-moon of missing teeth, and suggested what he obviously considered to be the perfect solution. Unfortunately, it came in a bottle.

After a polite pause, I graciously declined his offer of a drink. And then, on a whim, I decided to take the apartment. It had a certain *charme*. Even if it was the size of a post-it note.

I admit it is not quite the *appartement* I imagined living in, in the Paris of my fantasies. In fact, it barely even meets the description of a *boîte*—a box. It is more of a *folie*, really. A whimsical, *lunatique* idea that I wonder if I will regret when, some time down the track, I find that the toilet won't flush and the neighbours are all unstable.

Nevertheless, I can't help but love it. It has a certain endearing *simplicité*. It also has that other great property trait: location. You see, it is within a stiletto-throw of the best shoe shops in Paris and a gentle stroll from my beloved Luxembourg Gardens, so I don't mind if the bed nudges the kitchen and the only view is of my neighbours making love.

Each morning in this tiny apartment I rise at around six, thanks to the neighbourly alarm clock, which groans and moans and shouts, '*Oui! Oui! Oui! Ahhhhh ouuuiiii …*' without fail at quarter to five. I wash, which takes all of ten seconds because the bathroom sink is so close to my bed. I make a lukewarm *thé* from a kettle that doesn't work. And then I step out into the most glorious city in the world.

I head first to Poilâne, the noted *boulangerie*, where the famous *pain de campagne* is one part dough and three parts carbo-decadence, and buy a *pavé aux raisins* that's still warm from the oven. Then I return to St-Sulpice, marvelling at the beauty and the lines—the architectural ones as well as the *Da Vinci Code* ones—before making for the Luxembourg Gardens and a Parisian-style attempt at exercise. On the way, I usually stop at 6 rue Férou and pay my respects to the great Ernest Hemingway at his old address, and wonder what Ernest really thought when F. Scott Fitzgerald asked him to judge whether his penis was too small. (Apparently, it was the size of a hamster's.) Then, around mid-morning, I'll go and explore the streets of my quiet little *quartiers*, Odéon and St-Sulpice, and further north around rue Bonaparte and rue de Seine, pausing on the way to peer with pleasure into my favourite square, rue de Furstemberg. Occasionally I'll pop by the Musée Delacroix, which you reach via a series of enchanting courtyards, or stop at Karl Lagerfeld's gallery to see what splendid thing will be fashionable next. Sometimes I'll go to Odorantes, my favourite flower shop, which is barely bigger than a leaf but specialises in exquisitely beautiful bouquets that are organised by scent, and buy a little posy to brighten my minuscule studio. Other times, if I've bought a bouquet and still have money in my purse to spare, I'll have a cup of tea at Ladurée, the lavish French Chinoiserie-style salon. When I've done all that, I'll go and have a drink.

Now Paris is famous for idling at cafés and bistros, sipping on a kir, a delicious chilled white wine tinted pink with a splash of *cassis*, or blackcurrant liqueur. Unlike in LA, where everyone is in AA, there is no shame in asking for alcohol at one minute to midday. In fact, the city positively encourages it. Any Parisian doctor will tell you that a little *apéritif* or *vin rouge* is the best way to keep the heart pumping and the cheeks *framboise* with health. I am, sadly, not a big drinker (I say sadly because all my friends are), but I like the contemplation that comes with a small glass and a Parisian wicker chair. As one wit put it, 'I drink, therefore I think.'

For the last few weeks, though, I have been spending more time than usual in cafés and bars (well, usual for me—perhaps not for most Parisians) because I've been researching a story on the subject for a London magazine. 'All Bar Vin: Following in Hemingway's Footsteps' is to be a photographic feature on Paris's best drinking holes, although I don't know how clear the images will be after a solid week of alcohol. Nevertheless, I'm giving it my best shot (glass). Because how many other jobs are there where you can be paid to drink?

Now before you raise your eyebrows and roll your eyes let me reassure you of something. Researching a story on bars is hard work. Believe me. You see, first you have to drink. A lot. (Or in my case, learn how.) Once you've done this you have to recover sufficiently to do it all over again the next day. Just like Hemingway. Then, after

you've done this a couple of times, you're ready to go and do it in a real bar. I started this story years ago. I'm only just getting to the first paragraph.

Surprisingly, the hardest bit about writing a story on drinking isn't the drinking. Nor is it the description of the drinks (more on this later). It isn't even the painful recovery from the drinking. It's the *documentation* of it all when you've had three *pinots noirs* and are wondering if it isn't time to go home. Trying to decipher some illegible notes scribbled on a napkin is not easy. And it gets worse later in the day because by that time you've usually collected enough olive stains and Cointreau marks on your jeans to make your own martini. Not to mention the fact that the words have dribbled so far down the napkin they've run off onto a soggy coaster, which then gets lost beneath the mints in the bottom of your bag.

Finally, when you've think you've seen the bottoms of more glasses than Dean Martin and it's time to file the story you realise you can't remember a single quote, note or comment. Least of all your own.

I don't know how Ernest did it.

There are other important things to consider, too, when writing a bar story. Like drinking companions. These should be chosen, as Hemingway used to do, with great care, because it's highly likely not all of them will still be standing at eight pm let alone two am. And then the only contribution they're likely to make is a karaoke rendition of 'Roxanne'. Even when there's no karaoke machine.

And finally, there are the bartenders themselves. And this, I think, is where the secret to a good story lies. A good bartender can make a bar story brilliant. A bad one will just make you drunk. Last week I met a bad one. When it came time to leave the place it was all I could do not to slide off the chair and fall in a heap on the floor. It took me an hour to remember where I lived. And it was only a few doors away. When I did finally stumble home, I ran a bath, put on my favourite Frank Sinatra CD and didn't move again for three days.

I hasten to add that this isn't normal behaviour for me. My grandmother would have a fit if she thought I was wasting my life away on the Left Bank. It has only been for a few weeks. And I must admit I'm getting slightly weary of rocking up to a café, bistro or bar and feeling like a lush. To be honest, just the sight of an alcohol glass now makes me feel slightly ill and my cheeks go the colour of old *pelure d'oignon*, or onion peel.

Fortunately, Parisian cafés, bars and bistros are far more than just places in which to indulge in good plonk. They are charismatic vignettes of Parisian character, with personalities as distinctive as the alcohol they offer. And thus, they are the perfect places to sit and, like a good writer observing the world, while away the day.

Take the Crémerie Caves Miard, for example, a slice of conviviality on rue des Quatre-Vents in the sixth. In a space barely bigger than a cork from a Loire Valley red, former owner Pierre Jancou, who is almost as evangelical about creating a great space to drink as he is about serving natural, organic wines, transformed this late-nineteenth-century dairy into an atmospheric wine bar, retaining many of its original features so that what you get is a delightful sliver of turn-of-the-century charm. Think marble bench tops groaning with hams, rich timber shelves laden with organic reds and whites, delicious *saucisson* swinging above your head, and an original glass ceiling that's been untouched since it was put up in 1880. Quite simply, it's an architectural gem. Many locals love it so much they pop by simply to pick up a bottle for dinner and have a chat about vintages. I prefer to perch at one of the tiny wooden tables near the window, especially around lunchtime when exquisite little plates of organic tomatoes, aged parmesan, thin slices of Parma ham and other irresistible *charcuterie* slowly appear to help you wash down your glass of *Domaine Griottes*. With all the wines lined up like a still life behind me, an interior that makes me sigh from the sheer beauty of it and patrons who look like they also work in the media or fashion, with tailored jackets and funky scarves, I can't help but think that it's Paris as everyone imagines it to be. Hemingway would have loved it.

Although Ernest preferred a handful of Parisian cafés in which to write, arranging his surroundings as carefully as his blue-backed notebooks (they had to offer atmosphere while still being quiet and private: Hemingway abhorred any kind of distraction to his concentration), he always appreciated the merits of a well-designed café. For Hem, there was nothing more pleasurable than a place to sit and think. Preferably with a drink.

I have spent much of this afternoon ensconced in my little *crémerie*, chatting happily away in pathetic French with a forgiving Pierre and exploring the various *terroirs* of his favourite reds. I say much of the afternoon because I am still here, and who knows how long I'll be able to stay before Pierre kicks me out so he can lock up and leave? Usually he is more charming than a glass of his cheekily named *Pinoir de Soif* (Thirst Pinot), but I have seen him tighten with fury when he's displeased. And journalists aren't high on his list of favourite people. I heard that he once lost his temper with a writer from the *New York Times* when she took his photo without his permission. 'Madam,' he said in perfect English (and I can imagine him lowering a bottle and scowling at her as he did so), 'like an American Indian, if you take my picture I lose my soul.' I have been too scared to show my little SLR in the place ever since.

As I sit here, sipping on a glass of yellow *Quartz*, one of Pierre's fabulous finds, I look out into the fading light and wonder at the haunting magic that is Paris. Outside, the city is beginning to lose its leaves with the autumn chill and the footpaths glisten from a sprinkling of twilight rain. Locals continue to stroll in and out, asking for recommendations to drink with their veal or venison medallions. Some just want a hearty bottle of red to drink with their homemade *bouillabaisse* or *boeuf bourguignon*. Pierre, a top *négociant* (merchant) serves each with a jolly *bonjour*, giving them a peerless Muscadet, a Bordeaux or an impressive new Mondeuse wine, so they leave in spirited fashion, envisaging their dinner. 'Take, *enjoy!*' he says, handing a strongly clouded bottle of reddish brown *vin naturel* to two American tourists, who seem a little uncertain about the organic wine but utterly enthralled by the discovery of Pierre and this tucked-away gem. 'It is radical wine, but you will like it! Come back and tell me how it is tomorrow night.' And the two Texans leave, gratefully clutching their piece of liquid Paris.

I watch them wander down the street and then continue to write, jotting quirky notes about the city that I'll probably never need but feel compelled to record anyway.

All the way down the street, and in parallel boulevards from here to the Champs-Élysées, other people are doing the same in softly luminous havens, documenting stories and lives for books and diaries they may only read when they're old and frail and want to recall what their life was like when Paris was part of it. Bistros and bars are good for this. There is something irresistible about the sight of them and their beckoning warmth on a dismal night as the City of Light gathers up its day and readies itself for night. The misty spirals of breath from the first feel of chill act as a kind of signal to seek warmer environs—to tuck oneself into the embrace of an old banquette or timber chair and order up a rib-tickling-strong drink. The coffee machines sing; the smoke rises; the chatter increases to convivial levels. It's the hour of *l'apéro*. The drink.

I bought a beautiful little book once, *Authentic Bistros of Paris*, which claimed the soul of Paris was to be found in the city's bars and bistros. It was, it said, where the pulse of daily life kept time to the neighbourhoods' rhythms. From the first six am coffee and glance at the newspaper, kept folded behind the counter, to the first glass of white wine ordered at lunch to the parade of *apéritifs*; the *plat du jour*; the *digestif* at three pm, then the lingering atmosphere of evening, when the wines came out with dinner, the city's bistros and bars reflected the buzz, character and continuity of Parisian life.

Indeed, so many friendships and affairs have begun in front of a *guéridon*—that quintessentially Parisian round white marble table that rests out on the street terraces all over the city—that the manufacturers should install subtle advertising for things like discreet hotels, Viagra pills or weekend getaways.

Sitting in a Parisian bar is surely one of the most wonderful things to do in the world. The city may have changed since Hemingway kept office hours in the cafés of St-Germain, but there is still a little spirit, so to speak, left in Paris yet.

It is some time now since I arrived in Paris and I have settled into the city like an old soul, into a daily routine of writing stories, usually commissions for various magazines and newspapers, for several hours a day at one of my favourite cafés and then strolling the streets of Paris thereafter, finding solace among the beauty of the city's bewitching streets. I have started to feel the rhythms of the city and understand the different tempos of the Parisian day. The swanky department store that's Colette, where I venture to buy *branché* ('plugged in') magazines, mostly fashion and design titles, for an unsightly sum, no longer seems a strange mystery (although the one hundred different brands of mineral water still do), and I have stopped looking up for the sun in the mornings, knowing it has said *hasta la vista* for the autumn and winter and gone off to Ibiza.

Fuelled by a diet of salmon and salads from my favourite supermarket, a little too much *charcuterie* from my favourite *crémerie*, and of course the occasional champagne at one of my favourite bars, I have achieved a contentment that, I think, borders on happiness.

All around me Paris is wrapped up in its graceful coat of autumn, wonderfully beautiful. And, apart from the freak period that is the *métro* at peak hour, endearingly congenial.

I am beginning to feel at home.

Occasionally, however, and despite emails from friends all over the world, I do feel a pang of homesickness at times. After years of living in different places I thought I would be used to the gypsy life by now. I've always loved new places, meeting new friends, and tend to get bored if I stay anywhere for longer than a year. That's not to say I get bored with people—email is fabulous for staying in contact with friends and family—but I do get restless if I don't try something new.

There comes a time, however, when you wonder if life wouldn't be better lived in one place, with everyone you love around you. I'm sure this sentiment touches most of those who make their lives somewhere other than where their roots and families are, but it's still a shock to the psyche when it hits you.

This evening, having finally arrived home from the *crémerie*, I discover I have an email from my mother and it makes me particularly reflective. I have left several little nieces at home and she has spent numerous paragraphs regaling me with stories of their recent performances.

Not wishing to sink into a quicksand of melancholy, I decide that there is only one solution: the Parisian one—find a great Paris bar and order a glass of the finest bubbly they have. It doesn't matter that I am already feeling a little *entre deux vins* (between wines) or, as the French say, *pompette*—completely tipsy. All that matters is that I avoid that awful despondency known as expat homesickness.

I need help, however. So I call an old friend who has been idling in Paris for the past five years, working as a freelance writer for some of the world's best publications. Mark is used to the champagne life so I figure he will know just what to do. I also know that he has a liver like a blue whale, so an evening of alcohol-soaked hedonism won't pose a problem. As the French say, *il boit comme un trou*. He drinks like a hole.

I throw on a slash of slinky black jersey dress that I bought a decade ago but still love, because it's guaranteed to look half-decent even after a long night of cheap wine, and meet Mark at the one place I know we will be successful in dousing our expat cynicism. Le Fumoir.

Now there are some places in Paris you go to for romance or grandeur (Le Grand Véfour, La Tour d'Argent); others you go to for a celebrity perve (Alain Ducasse, L'Atelier); and yet others you stumble to when you want to keep drinking well after two am (Harry's Bar, Le Crocodile). And then there are some places you go with a journalist friend when you want, like Hem and Scott Fitzgerald, to have a good old writerly time. Le Fumoir is one of these. And not just because it offers a library of international newspapers to flick through if you grow bored with your companion.

An institution in Paris, this handsome 1940s-style smoking lounge opposite the Louvre has a stern, almost intimidating neo-colonial interior that belies the fun you can have here. There are well-worn leather chairs, a grand mahogany bar, oak furniture and ceiling fans whirring gently as if it is a foreign correspondents' club in Hanoi or Siem Reap. The waiters are straight out of an old French *film noir* and even the bar comes from a Chicago speakeasy. You couldn't get any more of a Baz Luhrmann–style interpretation of Paris if you tried. One website, worldsbestbars.com, describes it as 'smoother than [French singer] Sacha Distel's underwear'.

It is not part of the modern tableau of Paris—the fiercely slick bars with their minimalist postmodern interiors. Le Fumoir is very definitely part of the 'old Paris': the Paris that's glamorous and fabulous.

The secret with Le Fumoir is to embrace the gorgeous cliché of it all and surrender to the charm. Order a couple of martinis, flirt with the bartender and then weave your way to the library for an afternoon to remember. It's the kind of place where, as one journalist put it, you 'come for a cocktail and leave with a lover'.

I find Mark in the back, hiding behind a quiet Chablis and a copy of the London *Times*. The Chablis is almost taller than the *Times*. Mark is dressed to impress, in a black cashmere knit, black jeans and black Italian shoes. I feel my spirits begin to lift already. And I haven't even had a drink.

'Well, well!' he says, standing to greet me in gentlemanly fashion. 'If it isn't Ms McCulloch!'

Now the one thing you have to know about Mark is that he is more charming than a European prince. He could make a king look like someone you met at a suburban barbecue—six hours after it was time to go home. The man is Brad Pitt mixed with Matt Damon and then sewn into a Savile Row wardrobe. He could be a cad and you'd still fall for his grace and manners.

The other thing you should know about Mark is that he never drinks cheap booze. I can see that I'm in for a big night. Everyone should have one perfect drinking friend, the one who's useless in a crisis but fantastic when your bloodstream has such a high percentage of alcohol it's actually illegal, unless you're in the outback. Or Denmark. Mark is mine.

We start the conversation with an order for champagne, the drink of choice for discerning journos everywhere. At least modern ones. The old ones used to go for whisky but things have moved on. Mark deliberates between Krug (non-vintage) and a glass of Charles Heidsieck. I quietly ask for the cheapest one they have.

'*Oui, madame*,' says the waiter with no hint of patronisation whatsoever. Which makes me love him right from the start.

Now I hate to confess this, but I've never really understood much about champagne, except that it has bubbles and tastes nice. Once, an oenologist at a fancy soirée solemnly handed me a glass with the following instructions: 'I would normally give you something to eat, but with this particular champagne it's important to respect the equilibrium of the palate.' I was too ashamed to tell him that my liver absorbed alcohol so fast the palate was already sadly well gone.

Mark, fortunately, has far more of a grip on the situation and asks questions of the lovely waiter/sommelier that sound, to my ears at least, remarkably intelligent. I remain silent but nod at the right moments, feigning comprehension. When questioned as to the price range (just for research purposes, you understand), the diplomatic man doesn't reveal how much the bottles cost except to say that some are 'an even number between one and four with two noughts'. I can't conceive what this would be after three sips of potent bubbly so I merely nod again and take another sip. Ours tastes, as you would expect of a double-nought-priced number, very, very good.

'Did you know that there are about forty-nine million bubbles in a single bottle of champagne?' says Mark, studying his glass. 'And that the story of the shallow champagne glass being modelled on the breasts of Marie Antoinette is, in fact, untrue, since the glass was made long before, in 1663?'

'No, I didn't,' I say, already pleasantly sozzled and happy to believe anything he tosses my way. About breasts or otherwise.

'It was also the favourite drink of Napoleon and Josephine, and of Madame de Pompadour, who once declared that Moët & Chandon champagne is "the only wine that leaves women beautiful after drinking it".'

'Well, then,' I say, 'I'll drink to that.'

'*À ta santé* then!' replies Mark, raising his glass to offer a toast.

'*À tes amours*,' I say in return, toasting his loved ones, adding, '*À tes Cristal!*', which I think means, 'Let us drink to the company who created this fine liquid.' Or close enough to it, anyway.

An hour later, we are partners in champagne crime. And all I can think is: what a drink, and what a city this is. (Thankfully Mark is paying so I can think this without feeling sick.) There is further discussion about the magic of champagne, including discussions of top notes and aromas—I pick up snippets like 'mint, white flowers and citrus fruits'—and a debate on the complexity of a very fine silky Krug. But all I can do is sit back and absorb the liquid beauty of it all.

Now anyone who visits Paris knows that there are several complex things a foreigner faces in trying to navigate the social pitfalls of this city. The first is the people. But Parisians are easy to understand if you know the rules, and are polite, and considerate. This is their city, after all. Not ours. As much as we like to think it's for everyone. The second tricky thing, at least in my opinion, is the alcohol. There is much to drink in Paris, and it can be daunting finding your way around the glasses, dinner tables and bars if you don't know your Krug from your kir. In fact, if you don't order the right drink, or, indeed, if you grab the wrong glass at a dinner party by mistake, you may end up remembering (or not) the faux pas for a long time to come!

Parisians love to drink. A lot. Although there is now some talk about whether this is really just a myth stemming from years of good living. But it is certainly true that they love fine alcohol. Hang around Paris or a French person long enough and inevitably they will kindly offer you a glass of cognac, armagnac, Cointreau, or some other very fine shimmering liquid. Although France is known for its great champagne houses—Moët & Chandon, Krug, Veuve Clicquot Ponsardin, Bollinger and Louis Roederer—it is also famous for the drinks known as *digestifs*, which are made from sweet alcohol and flavourings such as fruit, herbs, spices, plants, flowers, seeds, roots and bark. Usually (although not always) served after a meal—because that is when you, and your stomach, are full enough to handle the alcohol content—these French after-dinner drinks are often 35 per cent proof.

(Not that you realise they are so potent until you wake up the next day and wonder where you've been for the past six hours. And why you're wearing someone else's stilettos.)

The most beautiful of these particular French drinks is cognac, which is a brandy that's produced in the region surrounding the town of Cognac, in south-western France. It is aged for at least two-and-half years in special oak barrels, which impart the cinnamon and vanilla flavours. What eventually evaporates from these barrels is described as *la part des anges*: 'the share claimed by the angels'. Cognac is usually double-distilled to achieve its legendary elegance and balance, and is rated in accordance with its origin and its age. The older the cognac, the better it will be. Just like French women.

At the elegant cafés on the rue St-Honoré, the glasses of Armagnac are so smooth, they're impossible to resist, even when you see the €29 price tag. Sip one and you feel immediately worldly.

Going down the scale, one comes to Cointreau, which is made by the Cointreau family who invented the eponymous liqueur in the mid-nineteenth century after a member of the family happened upon native wild oranges while on holiday in the Caribbean. Not wanting to send them home fresh, because they would have no doubt dried up during the long, hot voyage and thus caused consternation when they reached France, the gentleman organised for only the dried peels to go. Back home in France, his father, Edouard Cointreau, did indeed think his son was on some silly tropical juice when he sent the crate, and wondered if all the alcohol hadn't gone to his head in the sun. (Actually, I'm just making this up for the fun of it. But I'm sure he would have thought along these lines.) Being a thrifty businessman, however, Monsieur Cointreau took the strange, if highly aromatic, shipment of peels and experimented with them until he came up with the secret formula that is still used today. Ah yes, there's nothing like a holiday, even the inspiration of someone else's, to make you experiment with a little drink.

Finally, there is absinthe—more of an *apéritif* than a *digestif*—and a more wicked drink couldn't possibly exist anywhere else in the world. According to the wonderful food and wine blog www.davidlebovitz. com, this famous green-tinted hallucinogenic liqueur, which can have up to 72 per cent alcohol content (so much it is said to cause insanity), was supposedly used in the mid-1800s by the French army in North Africa as a health tonic to prevent disease and purify water. It was brought back to the cafés of *belle époque* Paris by those soldiers who had become quite fond of the taste, and very soon became the most popular aperitif in France, particularly among the bourgeoisie, who referred to their pre-dinner glass of absinthe as *L'Heure Verte*, the Green Hour. (I presume this refers to the colour of the drink and not the colour of your face the next day.) Immortalised in the paintings of artists like Manet and Toulouse-Lautrec, who referred to their liquid inspiration as the *Fée Verte* (Green Fairy) because they believed it gave them hallucinogenic visions, it soon became a legendary part of bohemian Paris in the late nineteenth and early twentieth centuries. Because of its potent qualities, however, it quickly came under suspicion from the government, and was eventually banned. Decades later, after almost a century of illegality, the government quietly lifted this ban in 1988, and the drink—true to its form—returned to the market with a bang. Parisians now love it, even though much of the older generation still think it's illegal. (But that only adds to the thrill of it, apparently.) It's a romantic tradition that entrances those who long for the heyday of artistic Paris, when sipping absinthe at a café in Montmartre was considered the epitome of great living.

Sadly, and quite ironically, considering the drink's renewed popularity, there are few places in Paris where you can actually try this wickedly suspicious elixir because the preparation that goes into it is quite complex. The Hôtel Royal Fromentin has a historic bar that serves it, as does a little bolthole called Vert d'Absinthe, at 11 rue d'Ormesson, which offers free tastings of different types. One pours water over a sugar cube in the glass of absinthe to make it cloudy (called *louching*), then imbibes the overpowering flavours of anise and spice, which are actually quite delicious. After the first sip, your tongue normally goes numb. After the second one you can no longer feel your mouth. And by the third sip time has well and truly stopped. The last time I tried absinthe, at a friend's apartment in the Marais, I couldn't move for several days.

'The world has gone mad,' said my friend finally, when we could feel and move our tongues enough to talk. I could only agree. Although I did wonder whether it was the world that had gone quietly mad—or whether it was just us?

But back to another very fine drink—my Fumoir champagne. After several hours with Mark and several bottles of something whose labels I can no longer read, I feel it is time to go home. My expat homesickness has well and truly been washed away, and I feel ready to take on another day of Parisian living. That is, if I can survive the night ahead.

I say my warmest goodbyes to Mark and, via a taxi that seems to go by way of Provence, return home to my little abode by nine pm. Sitting down at my desk, I have to increase the font size on my laptop four times because the desk is swaying. I wonder if Hemingway ever had this trouble.

An hour later, at ten, a girlfriend calls to see if I want to go for a drink. I explain that I'm already intoxicated enough but thank her profusely anyway, and add that even if I did fancy a glass of something light I would probably have trouble finding my shoes and making it out the door.

'Oh, that's a shame,' she says.

For a brief moment, I feel tempted. And then think of the comfort of bed.

That's the only problem with Paris. There are so many great bars you need to have a liver like Hemingway's to drink at them all.

I go to sleep dreaming strange dreams of glasses and corks and bars the size of Mars. But I no longer feel melancholy for home. All I feel, from my numb tongue to my tired toes, is the fabulousness and glamour of Paris.

. 5 .

Through Chic and Thin

THE ART OF GLAMOUR

It's amazing how many cares disappear when you decide
not to be something, but to be someone.

Gabrielle 'Coco' Chanel

It's five o'clock on a Friday night in a quiet street near St-Sulpice,
and, like many other Parisians looking forward to *le weekend*, I am
getting ready to go out for a drink. Outside, the night sky has already
changed into a denim blue and restaurants are re-dressing their tables
with freshly starched white linen and candles for the evening trade.
Paris has become a platform of visual seduction and it's difficult
not to feel the thrill and promise of what's to come. Brassaï, one of
Paris's great twentieth-century photographers, once wrote, 'the night
suggests, it does not show'. Paris is full of possibilities now the evening
has begun.

Tonight, Mark and I are having a small glass of something at
the Champagne Bar in Dokhan's Hotel, a sophisticated neoclassical-

inspired temple of high style where you feel compelled to dress up to sip your bubbly amid the stylish ones. Afterwards, we're meeting friends at a funky bar on St-Sulpice, where the interior is the size of the Mona Lisa but the industrial-strength drinks carry the weight of the I.M. Pei pyramid at the Louvre.

Young Parisians love to go out so much, there are now words to describe the various stages of the night: *le before* is the cocktail hour, when you prime yourself for the evening ahead; *le club*, naturally, is for when you're a little *pompette* and want to kick up your heels; *l'after* takes place around dawn, when you've had a few champagnes and start to think that your date is actually rather lovely and might be worth having breakfast with; and *l'after after* happens when the night stretches on until mid-morning, either from the adrenalin the diet pills have given you or because you've fallen head-over-Louboutins for the person you met way back at *le before*. There's even a phrase for the period after this, when you analyse the night you've had: *le brunch*, which is when you want to extend your Friday or Saturday-night date well into Saturday or Sunday. Or, indeed, Monday.

There's just one problem with all this *frivolité*, though, and it's the usual one: the small issue of what to wear.

This past month, as September drifted into October, a whole new style of fashion seems to have hit the stores of Paris: one based on the age-old art of seduction. Everywhere you look there are clothes that would make a grown man weak at the knees. There are theatrical black dresses that are drama redefined, ethereal grey chiffon evening gowns that put a new spin on the possibility of dancing, beautifully tailored suits that somehow capture the sexiness of 1940s Hollywood, and—most alluring of all—sublimely high shoes that offer a wicked thrill, in or out of the rest of your clothes. Designers have rediscovered the fading art of flirtation and glamour, and their collections are testament to the new love affair with sex.

Sadly, I don't have the funds to indulge in such decadent distractions,

and even if I did I probably wouldn't have any room in my apartment
to put them. For this and other reasons (a preoccupation with writing;
with the lack of babies and boyfriends; with life), my state of affairs
when it comes to style is, well, dismal. A few black wrap skirts, a few
cardigans (black, beige, pale pink, grey), a treasured black Armani
trouser suit that doubles for business and dates, two pairs of jeans,
some tailored Jigsaw jackets, one good dress (bought at a seconds store
in Knightsbridge), another Armani jacket (bought on sale on Regent
Street in a fit of madness), a few strappy dresses (origins unknown), a
red trench coat, and shoes that don't know which goes with what.

I've come to Paris to be glamorous. Or at least to be educated
in the art of glamour. And now my wardrobe is telling me, in no
uncertain terms, that *ce n'est pas possible*. It is nothing short of *une grande
catastrophe*.

I sneak a cigarette out of my secret supply and stand back to
survey my achingly empty *armoire*. The *armoire* just smirks back at me.
So I pour a 'boudoir drink' (a drink one has as one is dressing for the
evening) and wonder what to do.

While the bar around the corner isn't a problem, because you can
be naked and they'll still serve you an apple martini, the lavish decor of
Le Dokhan's is a slightly different affair. They expect you to be dressed
for the occasion when they dish up their heightened level of luxe. Jeans
will simply not suffice.

It's also now cool enough in the year to wear jackets and leather
gloves, but too hot in clubs and bars to look chic in cashmere or wool.
Which poses the problem: what to wear when you want to stay warm
on an autumn evening but still look sexy in a smoke-filled bar?

Ah, Paris. A city where the fashion issues never end.

When I first came to Paris, at the impressionable age of sixteen, the city seemed to be inhabited solely by fashionably thin, blazingly chic women wearing stylish trench coats with Marlene Dietrich–style insouciance and shoes so sharp they could have happily cracked off a heel and used it as a swizzle stick in their American martini. Everywhere I looked these luminous, pin-thin creatures rushed past, sporting alarmingly expensive crocodile skin handbags, pink or tomato red Chanel suits (it was the eighties, after all), and beautiful slingbacks, which they changed to simple black YSL-style trouser suits and even more beautiful stilettos in time for the five o'clock cocktail hour. Furthermore, each element, each heel, bag, jewel, lipstick and hair, was pulled together in such a way that they looked fiercely chic, severely beautiful and incredibly fragile all at the same time. Their expressions may have been reserved and composed but the reactions they invoked in others, including hot-blooded French men and impressionable young schoolgirls, was nothing short of shocking.

Needless to say, I was completely smitten, now as much as then. For a girl brought up in the country and then sent to a private girls' school with a famously strict uniform code (blazers worn at all times outside the school gate, long hair in neat ponytails and white knickers only, please), Paris was like entering another world. The city radiated style. Sex. Seductiveness. Luxury. Forget the Eiffel Tower. All I wanted to do was buy some decent lingerie to wear under my agnès b and sit in a café moodily discussing Sartre and Satie.

Twenty years on, little has changed. Parisian women are still thinner than a first-class plane ticket and shimmeringly chic. And the shoes they wear are still alarmingly fabulous. In fact, Parisian women are as pedantic about their clothes and shoes as they are about the lines of architecture framing the city. Just as what you read says volumes about who you'd like to be, what you wear paints a broad brushstroke of who you presume you are. Clothes talk. And you don't want them saying the wrong things.

Loulou de la Falaise, the French designer and one-time muse to Yves Saint Laurent, once said that French women are 'all entrance; effect; brilliance', and it is true. Paris is the city of *paraître*—appearance. Think of Chanel, Dior, Givenchy, Louis Vuitton, Yves Saint Laurent … It's gilt by association.

There is so much glamour seeping out of the avenues and stores it's enough to make you weak with envy every time you walk down the street. I thought I was perhaps close to having my own style when I left Australia and London. I thought, like most journalists working in magazines, I'd studied the rules and figured out all the answers. But any knowledge you think you may have pales into insignificance the moment you set foot in the City of Chic. Here you can be a beautifully dressed foreigner and still feel as though your slingbacks are all wrong and your lipstick is two shades too heavy—even if it is a Chanel.

Fashion matters to Parisians. Just as much as style and architecture. It's all part of *l'art de vivre*, the gentle art of living. And the sartorial judgment of others doesn't just stop at the fashion and design pack because even garbage workers, I've noticed, take a moment to assess the style parading down their streets. And they don't just wolf-whistle either. With solemn expressions, assessing people on their aesthetic QA, they look like judges on *American Idol*.

Because of this unspoken expectation to live up to *le non-dit*—the unsaid—Parisians loathe to be the only ones looking *de trop*. The worst kind of insult is for someone to consider your outfit with a slow look from head to toe and then murmur, 'Isn't what you're wearing a little … unsuitable?' Not that they would ever do that. Parisians are far too polite for that. They'd merely smile and then walk away making a mental note never to invite you over for tea.

Fashion is particularly important if you work in the French media, and absolutely crucial if you work in magazines. Few other things establish your credibility more than an awareness of the great art of tailoring. Plead ignorance of this and you may as well leave the country and go live in Alice Springs.

I had all these sartorial insights a few days after arriving in Paris on a previous visit when, quite by accident, I met a girl called Simone, who turned out to be a freelance stylist for some of the country's most respected fashion magazines. Paris, she said, can be a terrifying place if you can't speak fluent fashionese. I felt inclined to agree.

Learning the necessary social and style skills to navigate your way through any kind of new society is never easy, be it Sydney's magazine fraternity or London's royal circles, but tackling the chic clique of the Parisian set seems to require a whole different mindset. For a start, people view things differently here. They notice things in terms of colour or fashion references and can distinguish the difference between near-identical shades of grey. Such is their *sens esthétique* (aesthetic sense) that eventually some of it starts to rub off on you, and things you previously never considered suddenly become devastatingly important, such as which side you tie your trench coat on. (Tip: right is best.)

Tiptoeing through this stylish minefield was almost more than I could bear, and so one day I pleaded with Simone to fix my fashion inadequacies. Because her job involved writing about fashion, style and all the bits in between, I believed every word she said. Besides, who was I to argue with a girl who rotated three lovers on a fortnightly basis? She obviously had the art of *séduction* and glamour down pat.

And so with Simone at the helm, I've enrolled in an ongoing course on The Art of Parisian Chic, and How To Achieve It. I've become a fashion *flâneur*, strolling the stores, the boutiques, and the streets for a sartorial education. It's not as easy as you'd think. But as the old saying goes, *Il faut souffrir pour être belle*. You have to suffer, my girl, to be beautiful.

My first lesson in Parisian elegance was at a fashion show that Simone somehow managed to secure us tickets to. This was not just any fashion show, either, but one by the great Alexander McQueen, a designer so revered by every member of the media that whenever he does a show every fashion writer from Manhattan to Mumbai jumps at the chance to cover it. Famous for his flashy theatricality, the British designer's shows are filled with fantastic metaphors and fabulous allegories. And because of this, he guarantees glittering copy for those journalists who have to make a living out of writing about fantasies and imagery.

I was so excited I thought I might pee in my fake Prada pants.

When the week of The Show came around, Simone and I decided to meet inside, since trying to *rendez-vous* in a sea of photographers and steely journalists would be too difficult, we surmised, and require one of those handwritten cardboard signs you hold aloft at the airport. Not a good look when you're trying for chic.

Once the *rendez-vous* point was arranged, I turned my concentration to far more important things: planning what to wear.

A former editor once told me that the *sine qua non* of good style is a well-defined sense of understated luxury. Class, she said, comes not just from good bone structure and impeccable manners but a wardrobe that is expensive, yet inconspicuous. I remember looking in my minuscule wardrobe that morning and noting that the only thing inconspicuous was the lack of nice clothes.

It's a fashion truism that 60 per cent of what editors think about at these shows is what they're going to wear. What they do wear. What others are wearing. And what they should have worn. Everyone's looking at everything bar the catwalk. It's their job, after all. Theirs is the business of trafficking in taste. Sniffing out trends. Looking for the Next Big Thing. If Anna Wintour's wearing a beige trench coat, you can just about guarantee everyone else will have raced out and bought one before the next show has begun.

I once interviewed a famous British magazine editor who used to do the shows religiously year after year, sitting in the front row opposite

Anna Wintour, and she told me, with a certain amount of cynicism, that nearly all editors and the rest of those at the industry's pinnacle obsessed about clothes. 'The detail that goes into the planning before shows is extraordinary,' she said. It was, she added, about as neurotic as you can get. 'Everyone really does judge you on how you look,' she continued, sighing, obviously glad to be out of it all. 'It really is a nightmare. And whatever you pull out to wear, you always end up wishing you had worn something else.'

Her words didn't offer me any hope, less than three hours before the big show.

In the end, partly out of desperation and partly out of intoxication, because I had spent most of the morning drowning my nerves in a flat glass of champagne, I tossed on the only thing I thought would suit: my tailored black Armani pant suit, done in a soft tuxedo style, which I bought long ago in London when I seemed to have more money. I threw some pearl earrings in my ears, shoved my feet into some old heels and prayed it would suffice. I also prayed I could stand up straight after four glasses of flat champagne.

An hour later, I was weaving my way towards the show.

Simone, by chance, was out the front when I arrived, looking every bit a Parisian. She was dressed in a black satin trench coat, a killer black chiffon dress from Dolce & Gabbana and the latest black sandals from Dior. The whole look was very va-va-voom. I looked down at my low-key attempt at *luxe* and felt completely *déshabillée*. I knew immediately my sartorial education had a long way to go.

Inside, we were greeted by a cool publicist in gunmetal grey, who looked at us with barely a flicker of a smile ('It means we are accepted,' said Simone behind her back) and ushered us into the cavernous space, to chairs that were so far back I thought she had ushered us right into the toilets.

And then the most extraordinary thing happened. Barely a second later we were tapped on the arm and told to move further up the front

by a man who looked like he knew what he was doing. Not wishing
to argue, we followed him. All the way up to one of the front rows. It
wasn't quite row B (row A is for celebrities and Anna Wintour) but it
was still within the alphabet. And away from *les toilettes*.

I desperately tried to look world-weary and unimpressed but inside
I was faint with terror. And because all fashion shows start late I was
rigid with fear that someone would notice I wasn't actually A Very
Famous Journalist and usher me back to *le pipi-room* again.

Beside me Simone drifted into boredom and started writing out
a list of Things To Do. Around us, the veteran fashionistas filtered in
and seemed to do the same. There's obviously nothing like the fashion
shows to catch up on a bit of notepadding action. Others folded their
programs and starting fanning themselves as if to say, 'God, I'd rather
be in Bali.' Raw with fear, I tried to copy them.

Next to me, two well-known editors in top-to-toe black (it is still *de
bon ton* to wear black, I noticed with relief) started discussing *le peeling*
and *le lifting* and *le tuck-'n'-trim* (in more places, too, than just their eyes
and breasts), with the kind of ennui that comes after you've become
so *au fait* with your plastic surgeon, he's now on your dinner party list.
I knew it was terribly bad mannered to eavesdrop but I couldn't help
it. I was enthralled.

Despite the world-weariness of these wanderers, however, a certain
underlying excitement was starting to creep into their conversations,
and the sea of aesthetics that surrounded them. Rumours about the
show being one of the best had already leaked out to the press and
every editor and every photographer, even those at the very back, was
secretly on high alert. You could sense the Manolo Blahniks tap-tap-
tapping impatiently on the bare wooden floor.

Finally, the lights dimmed and the show began.

High on stamina and low on fat, the models paraded out one by
one, dressed in clothes that were glamorous but sometimes so brief
you didn't know where to look. The photographers, naturally, knew

La Vie
Parisienne

just where to train their experienced eyes, and swivelled their lenses straight to the good bits.

As the music soundtrack segued from classic to rock-pop and then seventies disco, the models who started out as beautifully dressed mistresses eventually ended up as undressed whores, wearing little but shoes and a grin.

The editors, of course, loved it. 'Oh!' they exclaimed, crying into their Dior handbags. 'Such *élan!*'

Unfortunately, I couldn't see Alexander's *élan* because I was too busy being horrified by the buttock cracks exposed by the low-slung jeans of the celebrities in front of me. But I could hear the cheers through my new friends' *derrières*.

'*Bravo!*' the editors cried, gathering around Alexander like flies. '*Bravo!*' And then they all stumbled out of the place so fast I thought a Chanel sale had been announced.

I felt like I needed a cup of tea and a long lie down.

'I think I'm getting a headache,' said Simone, pressing her temple. I wearily agreed.

Half an hour later, we had removed ourselves from the stylish scrum and ensconced ourselves in the chic comfort of the Hôtel Costes on St-Honoré, which is loved by the fashion pack for its rich *fin-de-siècle*-ness, where we proceeded to order a Veuve to steady our nerves. I was still suffering from shock so I ordered a G&T as well, and then vodka straight up.

'What did you think?' Simone said, after I'd sculled a glass.

'Beautiful,' I nodded enthusiastically, not really sure what it was all about but feeling that I needed to give it the thumbs up nonetheless.

'Mmm.' She shrugged. 'It was good. A little … *dépassé* in places. But yes, very good.'

'*Dépassé?*'

'You know. *Démodé* … Some of it was, mmm, a little last year? But the rest, it was *magnifique.*'

'Oh,' I said, wondering how a trend could be over before it left the catwalk.

And then my stylish friend, perhaps realising that I was floundering badly on the subject of fashion and needed immediate assistance, decided to fill me in on a few French secrets.

'These *prêt-à-porter* shows, they're not about the clothes you know,' she said, raising her head and staring at me earnestly, as if she was about to reveal some small but profound snippet of French wisdom.

'No?' I said, perplexed

'*Non*. They are about *la fantaisie*. The *hoopla* and glamour and the *imagination* of it all. Nobody is going to wear these clothes straight from the catwalk. You have to 'calm them down' with more normal things. They're more about the *fantasy* of fashion.'

I thought of McQueen's elaborately conceived costume dramas and thought that perhaps she had a point.

'That's all these fashion shows are. Figments of the couturiers' imaginations. They are *fantasies*.' She took another sip of her drink and shrugged. The gesture was so very Gallic I instantly decided that I wanted to learn to shrug like that.

'And anyway,' she continued, 'even if they were wearable … well it does not matter, because nobody is seeing the clothes. They are all too busy seeing who is in the front row. Celebrities are the new attraction at fashion shows. Nobody cares what the models are wearing. They just want to see Beyoncé and Kylie Minogue.'

I had to admit she was right. I had barely noticed what was happening on the catwalk. I had been too busy ogling at the editors and celebrities. The girls could have indulged in a lesbian romp and most of us would still have been fixated on Anna Wintour's bob.

Recently, I had another opportunity to further explore the secrets of glamour when I met up with my new friend Alexandra, whom I met when I spilled wine on her Marni jacket at a Left Bank book reading one evening, a long time ago. Alexandra is a book editor but she should have been in magazines. The girl is a walking *Vogue* cover.

It was a beautiful autumn day, a day for analysing the intricacies of style. We met at Spoon in the eighth, which is Paris's answer to whimsy. The brainchild of Alain Ducasse, the emperor of *haute cuisine*, it is one part *Wallpaper* magazine–style wit and one part navel-gazing solemnity. The cutlery includes chopsticks, china spoons or conventional knives and forks (you choose) and the décor doesn't know whether to lean towards self-deprecating and fun or sit up straight and act in a proper and dignified manner. The clientele, of course, take it all in their Parisian stride, and think it's simply chic. I think it's delightful, if you don't take it too seriously.

Alexandra, who was already there when I arrived, was wearing Chloé, the label of choice for every Left Bank A-lister. I was wearing jeans, the label of choice for every poor writer. She had paired her Chloé dress with big smoky eyes, a big chocolate leather belt and high-heeled chocolate boots. It was very French. I couldn't help but be impressed.

I have decided that there is a special dietary regime all Parisian women follow: that is, buy the clothes you want to fit into—Chloé, Chanel, those miniscule La Perla knickers—and then diet like the devil to do so. The clothes act as an incentive, you see. Who's going to let Chloé go to waste in a wardrobe?

I have also ascertained that French women smoke a lot. Far more than Australians, Londoners or LA girls. And they drink a lot of espressos too, almost as often as their Hollywood counterparts drop diet pills. All this caffeine and nicotine acts as a stimulant, enabling them to undertake marathon workouts—walking up and down hundreds of stairs, racing all over the city on foot and bedding a list of lovers—with the kind of energy that would impress the Tour de France entrants.

I am determined to adopt the same lifestyle.

Unfortunately, those of us who believe French chic is achieved through a diet of café noirs, Chanel suits, naked lovers and Gauloises will never really achieve true French style, according to Alexandra. French women do not look the way they do by relying on classic French tailoring and a no-fat, caffeine-filled diet with a Frenchman on the side. Although these things help, she adds. Nor do they achieve legs as slender as a Louis XVI salon chair by snacking on foie gras and sucking a nightly bottle of Beaujolais.

Non. What French women have mastered, argues Alexandra, is something the rest of us are still desperately trying to master: namely, the art of sartorial discipline.

'French women always make sure they are *coquette*, which means being well groomed,' said my friend, sitting prettily in her café seat with a poise that would have impressed the Queen. 'They always make sure that they have the right lipstick and the right accessories to match, and that their shoes have been polished no less than three weeks ago.'

Three weeks, I gulped silently. I had shoes in my parents' wardrobe back home in Australia that I hadn't seen for three years.

'We learn to coordinate at a very young age,' she finished solemnly.

'How?' I said, thinking back to my childhood and recalling nothing but horse riding and country parties when the boys tried to rip your knickers off, not comment on their labels.

'Ah, well this is an art that's passed down through the generations,' she said. 'My mother taught me everything. She told me I had to have one nice coat for work and another for winter and a dress for dinner, and with each outfit you had to have the shoes to match the bag.'

'What happens if you don't?' I asked nervously, trying to hide my mismatching shoes and bag under the table.

'Well, you do. Otherwise, you will get a bad name. You have to respect certain codes in France. Fashion is very important, *n'est-ce pas?*'

'*Oui*,' I agreed dismally.

Later that day, I strolled Paris's most famous fashion landmarks, making a mental note to wear more comfortable shoes next time I did so. (Ballet flats are adored in Paris for this very reason: you can wear them under jeans or skirts and race all over town while still looking like Audrey Hepburn in *Funny Face*. Well, almost.)

The first stop was le Bon Marché, or 'le BM', as the French call it (pronounced *bay-em*), which is where both the ladies who lunch and those who just have lovers go to replenish their tasteful wardrobes.

Five minutes into the store and I was already feeling the pull of French style, having discovered a wickedly pretty but sinfully expensive skirt and a sexy black strapless dress that would have impressed Sophia Loren. Unfortunately, they were both so expensive they would have pushed me into the league of the dishwasher like poor George Orwell, and I would no doubt have had to resort to washing dirty dishes for the rest of my life to pay for them. (Although I would have been very stylish while I scrubbed the pots.)

Dejected, I wandered into the fragrance area to spray some Chanel No. 5. If there is one thing guaranteed to make you feel Parisian, it's fine French perfume. It has always distinguished a woman from a crowd. (When the French royal family tried to flee France disguised as commoners at the height of the French Revolution, they were betrayed by Marie Antoinette's perfume, which ordinary citizens didn't wear.)

Smelling like Marie Antoinette, I ambled up to rue du Cherche-Midi to find some new shoes, since the ones I was wearing were giving me facial expressions that weren't very French. I couldn't find any comfortable shoes but I *did* spot a sublime pair of stiletto heels that were cheap(ish), if you consider anything under €200 a good price. Sadly, they were also a size too small. But I didn't care. I had to have them. I paraded up and down the store in them, gazing down at their delicate beauty and rationalising price versus pain. As I walked and contemplated, walked and contemplated, the salesgirl eventually raised her eyebrows and then gave a sort of French grimace, which seemed to suggest the image I gave off wasn't doing anything for her.

'Madame,' she said pointedly, 'these are very beautiful shoes, *oui*, but it does take a certain …' she paused, 'style to carry them off.'

I stared at her.

'*Sans aucun doute*,' I said coldly. 'Undoubtedly. I'll take them.'

To my surprise she said nothing. (Although I don't think her Botoxed forehead could have raised a crease.) She merely bagged them up without a word and handed them to me with only a slight shift of the shoulders.

'*Bon après-midi*,' she said mildly, probably glad to be rid of the gauche foreigner with her ugly heels.

Full of confidence I donned my beautiful new shoes and decided to head straight out to Dior before my new French-style bravado escaped me.

Now Dior is one of the most decadent, deliriously beautiful fashion stores you could have the privilege of stepping into. The changing rooms are dressed in padded satin and trimmed with bows and the whole mood of the place is one of refined luxury and quietly exchanged credit cards. If you're not married to a French banker and therefore accustomed to seeing lots of noughts on the end of your bank statements, however, the price tags can make you feel faint, and taking deep breaths before you put your head between your knees is not a good look in the middle of Dior.

They will, however, respect you if you are well groomed, particularly if you have a decent haircut and are wearing good shoes and a stylish handbag. Luckily I was. My new shoes made me new friends in Dior faster than a poodle looking for a doggy liaison in the Luxembourg Gardens.

I browsed for a little while, trying to act as if I schlepped in and out of here every day, and then, with a polite '*Merci, madame, au revoir,*' casually waltzed out again, taking deep gulps of air to revive myself. Revitalised by a swig of free water from my recycled water bottle and an old mint I found in the bottom of my handbag, I consulted the rest of the entries in the list Alexandra had graciously given me.

Under the headline *Magasins à visiter pour assurer la sophistication française* (Stores to visit to ensure French sophistication), she had written: Christian Louboutin, Sergio Rossi, Lucien Pellat-Finet, Petit Bateau, L'Eclaireur, and something called the 'Bob Shop', which sounded like a rather dubious place where you'd either pick up second-hand camping gear or cast-offs from the wardrobes of deceased estates. I didn't fancy wearing a pair of hiking boots nor someone else's sweaty old 1920s cardigan—and besides, I didn't think either would look very French—so I crossed that off and considered the rest. And then, feeling slightly dazed at the prospect of yet more potentially intimidating sales assistants and more horrifically expensive price tags, I looked up, saw the Café de Flore and decided to stop and have a little drink to help ease the pain of it all. Besides, I had a pair of beautiful new shoes to tend to. I didn't want to wear them out on the very first day. I had to show them off, even if it was only to the waiters.

Later that afternoon, as I stumbled over another cobblestone in my chic new heels, I started to think about glamour, and what we females did in the name of it. Joan Crawford used to change her outfit as often as ten times a day to achieve her particular shoulder-padded style of glamour. And Gloria Swanson—a woman who once said, 'When I am a star I shall be every inch and every moment a star'—used to stay in the Hôtel de Crillon but rent a townhouse for her wardrobe because the Crillon felt 'too cramped' for her three hundred dresses. Now that's glamour. How did one learn such an art? I wondered.

I didn't know. All I knew was that Paris was the last bastion of it. And that my pretty new heels were killing me.

Naturally, all of this fashion talk continued to bother me, in the same way that a new shoe rubs on an old ankle blister. Like any journalist, I felt I had to get to the bottom of it. And I had to do it soon. Before I was tossed out of Paris on a charge of bad taste.

So, after weeks of listening to lessons on the art of style and getting absolutely nowhere, I decided to call someone who would really know: an Australian girlfriend, Emily, who had been living in Paris for much of the past year. She would have experienced the same sartorial struggle, I figured. And I hoped she would, by now, have mastered all the answers.

Ironically, the last time I had seen Emily, in a café in North Fitzroy, she had been more anti-glamour than Germaine Greer. But then one day, out of the blue, she decided to pack up her hemp pants and jump on the first cheap Vietnam Airlines flight to Paris. I think she was meant to study or write for some organic farming magazine or something, I forget which, but instead of advocating the advantages of waste reduction, she discovered the frivolities of fashion. Shortly afterwards, according to a mutual friend, she ditched the clogs for Christian Louboutins, replaced cotton with cashmere, and could be seen sauntering down the street in a wave of Guerlain. The girl not only crossed the tracks, she changed demographics altogether. If there were a new religious cult called Pradaism she would have been its number one supporter.

I was curious to see how she had changed.

To Emily's credit, she sounded pleased to hear from me. We arranged to meet earlier at her boyfriend's apartment on rue

Bonaparte, before heading to L'Atelier de Joël Robuchon for a catch-up gossip and a quick bite to eat. I had heard that her boyfriend was a philosopher or a professor of philosophy or something and so half-expected an academic-style den, full of books with parchment covers and prints of maps on the walls. However, the interior was all steel and glass, with flashes of black stone, like some fabulous, bejewelled Georg Jensen design. It was also completely bare except for a grey *chaise* and a showpiece Bang & Olufsen sound system, which not only stood as a modern exclamation mark but made the sense of space even more hauntingly hollow. It was almost the ultimate Paris luxury: an enormous apartment with nothing in it.

I didn't know where to look first—seeing as there wasn't a lot to look at. So I perched on the end of the uncomfortable grey *chaise*.

'Don't mind the mess!' said Emily apologetically, waving airily at the monastic surrounds.

'Okay,' I replied, feeling distinctly in need of a cushion.

We headed to Joël Robuchon's new restaurant, which is one of the most fashionable tables in Paris, even though there are no tables to speak of, just a minimalist bar and so few stools that a kind of musical chairs goes on each evening between diners wanting to sit.

Emily ordered for us both, choosing the tapas from the menu. I looked at the prices and felt slightly nauseous. Organic farming media must be well paid, I thought.

'It's lovely to see you again after all this time!' I said, thoroughly meaning it.

In her tightly glamorous Chanel, she was the epitome of chic indifference. She'd also picked up, I noticed with a journalist's discerning eye, that studied nonchalance many Parisian women brandish like a suit of sartorial armour. The girl would have made Coco proud.

Next to us, immaculately dressed *petites filles* played absent-mindedly with their forks before putting down their napkins and pushing their plates away. This was obviously what you did in Paris to stay thin.

To make matters worse, the restaurant had been designed in such a way that the seats were excruciatingly uncomfortable. By the time our starters came around, I was ready to go home. The fabric of the afternoon only slackened when the plates were cleared and tea was poured. I took a sip of mine, which felt cold somehow. Unlike the atmosphere, which had turned distinctly humid. I could feel my woollen cardigan start to itch.

I thought Emily might have given me some tips on the art of style, but so far she had revealed nothing. Not a *saucisson*. In this way, she had turned completely French.

'You know I don't really eat,' she said suddenly, as if I hadn't noticed. 'You can't eat in Paris. Everything is full of carbs. Everything is white.'

'White?' I was confused.

'You know, white baguettes, white croissants, white cakes … It's crazy. I don't know how they go to the toilet! I love this city but the food is so rich. And anyway, even if you could find a restaurant that sold healthy fare here you couldn't eat it because then you'd never fit into your Chloé.'

And there it was. The secret to French fashion. Don't eat and you'll look chic within a few weeks. That is, if you haven't fainted from exhaustion first.

'You know, it's very important to look chic in Paris,' she finished, employing a more serious note as we toyed with our teacups.

'Yes, I've heard,' I said dryly, trying to keep the sarcasm from my tone.

But she looked solemn as she reached for her purse. 'In this part of Paris, and especially in the media and publishing worlds, everything rests on what you wear. Really, Janelle. Nothing could be more important.'

Her advice rang in my ears long after I kissed her goodbye and left her to her sartorial ways. I couldn't help but think that she was right, and that it was almost as imperative to learn the art of dressing in Paris as it was to learn the language.

And so, with Emily's warning ringing in my ears, I decided to embark on further learning—which I knew would be something of a vertical curve—in order to become truly *au fait* with the art of glamour and style. With the help of Alexandra and Simone, I became a student of shape, form, silhouette and line. I reread Diana Vreeland, watched DVDs of Audrey Hepburn and memorised the mantras of Chanel (always take one thing off before you leave the room ... and that doesn't mean your knickers). After a couple of days, I felt that I could just about go one-on-one with Madame Gabrielle herself (a woman for whom the armholes held the key to a perfect suit). I was close to being, if not *soignée*, then certainly seductive. Or so I thought. I had achieved what the Italians call *il sentimento dell'eleganza*: a sense of elegance. Even though my bank account was as flimsy as the latest Prada frock.

The most wonderful website I came across in this search for French style was a blog called *Tongue in Cheek*, which was an assortment of stories collected by a girl called Corey Amaro, a foreigner now living in France. Under the heading 'How to Dress like a French Woman', she had listed various tips, including wearing sexy lingerie, red gloves and different fragrances for different times of day. She had also suggested standing tall and, when you couldn't tie your scarf in the French fashion, undoing your top button instead, and calling it a day.

I thought it was magnificent. I learned more reading this list than I did in an hour of strolling around Chanel.

But what French glamour and fashion really comes down to, I learned, is the art of hiding everything so that all that remains is a little 'mystique'. The English, Americans and Australians wear everything on their shoulders so that their style is put out there for all to see. It's blatant and in your face. The French, on the other hand, never give anything away. Style is a wink, a nod, a tip of the hat to fashion and fads, but never a full exposé. It doesn't do to be totally transparent. In Paris, *transparence* is a dirty word. The worst fear of *les filles françaises* is to look vulgar and try-hard. The line between 'sexy and seductive' and 'trampy and sad' is very fine, but it is still a line.

'Of course,' said Simone, when I questioned her about it one evening over a coffee, 'French people don't talk about or wear fashion in the same way that you English do—we don't go on and on about the new look or the new shape. We know that certain things are in fashion but we are happy wearing what we wear—which is the classic French look. Most Parisians wear the same pieces season after season: a trench coat, a pair of beautifully cut trousers, perhaps a cashmere sweater, beautiful shoes, a good handbag and, yes, good lingerie. Sometimes we dress it up with a necklace or a pretty scarf. But we would never—*never*—want to look like one of those—' she shuddered, 'gauche Hollywood starlets. Those girls who always look undressed. Just remember, good fashion, or style, is about elegance, and elegance comes from hiding a little.'

Thus ended my lesson in the art of Parisian style. Apart from one little thing. 'Oh, and I almost forgot to tell you,' added Simone as I got up to pay for the coffees, 'don't smile. People don't smile in Paris unless they know you. It makes you look like a foreigner. *Regardez.*' She adopted a funereal expression. 'See?' She kept staring emptily at me.

No, I didn't. But I nodded anyway. And then adopted an expression Dirty Harry would have been proud of.

None of these lessons are coming close, though, to helping me this evening, as I prepare to dress for Dokhan's Hotel.

All my life, I've worried about what to wear. Blame it on growing up in the country and being sent to a city girls' school, then choosing an industry where what's on your back is often considered more important than what's in your mind. The pressure to be aesthetically perfect is disconcerting at the best of times, but when you work in magazines it becomes a deeply depressing concern. For years, I have worried that I don't measure up; that my highlights and handbag and heels are all wrong, and that one day I'll end up stumbling over a style divide and losing my footing on the wrong kind of shoe. But mostly I wonder if, when you work so hard to be someone else, do you eventually forget who you really are?

Now that I've come to Paris all these deep-seated anxieties are coming to the surface, and the flaws in the façade are starting to show. I can't help it. The trouble with being in another city and wanting to reinvent yourself is that sometimes the old you still shows through, muddying the grand plan. As much as I'd like to be the kind of person who considers these issues with gravitas and never walks out the door in anything less than a Dioresque silhouette, I fear that I am, and will always be at heart, an Australian girl from the country. And when it comes down to it: we simply don't give a damn. We like authenticity over flashy glamour and will take what's in a person's heart over what's on the back of their designer pants any day.

I sigh heavily. And then sigh heavily again. All this pressure and tension is making me feel slightly ill. It's worse than studying for the final year exams at university.

Outside the night is getting darker and the weekend frivolity has begun. It's one of those splendid evenings that's still warm, and full of the smells of autumn: *bouillabaisse* and warm baguettes and *bisque de homard* (lobster bisque). And here I am, still hopping from one foot to another in my knickers and bra.

I look out the window at my Parisian neighbour wandering around her equally tiny apartment. Her amorous other half isn't there and the night feels strangely quiet without him. She, too, seems at a loss for what to do. She pours a red and picks up a postcard from the bench. Her hair is a glamorous mess, as if she's just absent-mindedly pulled it out of a chignon, but her nails are still immaculately done and her slip and knickers look much more refined than mine, I note with dismay. Nevertheless, she looks unsure of herself, and lights a cigarette before staring into space.

And then it occurs to me: we are, all of us, unsure in one way or another. Few of us have life sorted in just the way we want. We are all driven by fear and anxiety and needs, even if we don't like to admit it. Clothes are simply our way of fortifying ourselves against the world: creating an armour of glamour that allows us to act a little more confidently, suggestively, provocatively, professionally. When we're not wearing our armour, we feel naked. In more ways than one.

For this reason, we often put too much pressure on clothes: pressure they can't always withstand. We give them the responsibility of making us look confident, clever, sexy, professional, when sometimes it's all they can do just to keep us respectably decent and suitably warm. Our poor clothes bear the brunt of all our insecurities and anxieties when really it is our inner style and strength that should be enhancing their tailored lines. It's not our clothes that make us who we are: they simply frame our personalities. It's actually the person inside who brings out the character and glamour.

Thinking of this, I tug on a floaty pink skirt, slip on a fitted jacket and tuck my feet into a much-loved pair of mules. Then I do my makeup, and, taking at last look at my neighbour redoing her nails (still looking far more glamorous than me), head out the door.

Sometimes the trick is in picking out your favourite outfit and then letting your personality do the rest. When it comes down to it, Parisian glamour isn't that hard to do. You just need a little bluff. And a bit of self-respect. In the words of Coco Chanel: 'Look for the woman in the dress. If there is no woman, there is no dress.'

In the salon of Dokhan's Champagne Bar, amid the distinguished absinthe-green timber panelling, distinguished remnants of the eighteenth-century rescued by Frédéric Méchiche and restored for the decadence of today, I ask Mark why fashion and clothes have come to mean so much to one city. With the walls dripping of glamour around us, it seems a suitable place to ask such a question.

He raises his glass and takes a sip before answering. *'On est toujours prêt!'* comes the reply. 'Because one is always ready.'

'For what?'

'For taking those clothes off,' he says with a wink.

. 6 .

Le Boudoir

BETWEEN THE SHEETS

It's true that the French have a certain obsession with sex,
but it's a particularly adult obsession. France is the thriftiest
of all nations. To a Frenchman sex provides the most
economical way to have fun.

Anita Loos

In Paris there is an appropriate and an inappropriate way to
do everything, and not just when it comes to style. There is an
appropriate handbag (which isn't Hermès, by the way, because too
many Americans buy it); an appropriate 'look' (anything with a slim
cut that's black, beautifully made and expensive); an appropriate
drink (usually wine, unless one is celebrating or commiserating, in
which case it is champagne), and an appropriate way to drink it (you
have to wait until all the guests have arrived—swigging a bottle in the
kitchen over the *tête de veau* to help you cope with the night ahead is
not considered elegant behaviour).

The only time Parisians like to be inappropriate is when they're having sex, when, to the surprise of many foreigners, they do things the Scandinavians would find shocking. In fact, in Paris infidelity is part of the fabric of life—the dirty bits are what they live for. There is even a time of day devoted to it—*cinq à sept*, from five to seven, known as 'the hours of the mistress', after which it's time to go home to the wife.

It's slightly mischievous behaviour that doesn't quite seem to fit with the rest of the bourgeois lifestyle. But then, this social dichotomy is all part of the French charm. You can be coquettish and a courtesan at the same time and no one will mind in the least.

As you can tell, this chapter's about Parisians and sex. Actually, perhaps I should rephrase that. It's about foreigners and Parisians and sex. Because it's not French people who are obsessed with sex (a study by French sexologists found that 50 per cent of French people couldn't care less if they went without sex for several months), but us foreigners who are obsessed with the French *having* sex. For some reason, we believe that the French have more sex than the rest of the world. And it fascinates us.

Mind you, this curiosity has lurked in the western subconscious for years. The books of the Marquis de Sade, a gentleman who knew all about *Le Hard*, still continue to sell centuries after he finally submitted to *Le Soft* and passed on to that big after-party in the sky. And when Catherine Millet, a magazine editor, intellectual and libertine with a ferocious appetite for *la partouze* (which roughly translates as, well, you know …) penned her erotic memoirs the rest of the world rushed to buy the million copies the publisher pumped out. No pun intended.

The French, of course, don't help the situation by producing films that are only just this side of pornographic. (Tastefully pornographic, but full of erect bits just the same.) Indeed, such is the fascination with the collective libido of this Latin country that all the dirty words seem to have sprung from the language: French kiss, French sex, *folie à deux*, *ménage à trois*, *ménage à soixante huit*. If you haven't travelled there, you'd think the place was heaving with pleasure.

Yet the reality is, according to well-researched stats and studies, the French have sex as infrequently as the rest of us. One study found they had it less than the Japanese, which, when you consider Japanese work hours, is saying a lot.

So why all the fuss?

Well, one French friend of mine, Jean-Louis, who sells me my fruit each day from the market on rue de Buci and occasionally has a coffee with me when his stall is quiet, says it's all to do with the age-old argument of quality rather than quantity.

'The French—with the exception of Catherine Millet—may not do it as often as everyone thinks, but when we fuck, we fuck with finesse,' he told me one day, calmly peeling an orange. (For a country that places so much importance on *la politesse*—or etiquette—they're decidedly nonchalant about tossing around the f-word.) 'Sex, like any other creative pursuit,' he continued, 'is an art form. And, as the rest of the world knows, we French love an art form!'

He went on to explain that, while I come home and have a red at the end of the day, he comes home and has a red and a blonde and a brunette too. At least I think that's what he said.

'I have a reputation to uphold, after all,' he finished, shrugging and devouring the orange in one impressive mouthful before adding with a wink: 'There is a great French saying: home is where another man's wife is …'

He was so comfortable with the conversation; it was as if we were chatting about the price of apples at the organic produce markets.

'*Oui, bien entendu*,' he shrugged again when I asked them if these sorts of things—threesomes and eightsomes and collecting mistresses like mineral water—really happen. 'Of course. *C'est normal*.' And then he excused himself, no doubt to go and shag his lover.

It was then I realised something. It is not the scandalous acts themselves that makes the rest of us curious—although they, too, pique our interest—but the French people's healthy attitude to it.

We envy their ease with it all. We wish that we, too, could strip off and engage in things that would make a street girl blush. We wish we could be Betty Blue, flouncing around in our birthday suits. And a great many of us would love to embark on a lifelong study of sexual gratification until we're expert on erotic aestheticism and can write filthy literature, highbrow or low, that would make our grandmothers turn in their graves.

Of course, something always stops us—usually our Anglo-Saxon prudishness. But that doesn't mean we don't devour whatever French sex we can, even if it's only in the form of literature or film. We may not have the courage to slide between the Egyptian cotton sheets but we're sure lifting them up to have a look.

You know what the best thing about all this French-style voyeurism is though? There are no agonising preambles. You don't have to wade through scenes of fluff to get to the good stuff. (When friends of mine read *The Bride Stripped Bare* they didn't even bother finding out the plot: they just skipped to the filthy pages. An underground tube journey is only so long, after all.) In most good French films or books, they just take off their kit and step right in. Forget the plot, says the director; let's go straight to the sex scene. And we lap it up gratefully. And then sneak back for seconds.

Of course, all this sex talk has does wonders for French tourism. There's nothing like the libidinousness of fantasising about a Latin lover to create a potent advertisement for a country. I know people who have jumped on a flight to Charles de Gaulle after two scenes of *Madeline*. (Even the teachers are sexy, you see.) Personally, I have always preferred Italian men. But I can understand the appeal of the French man. I would most likely do the dirty with Gérard Depardieu too, if I had the chance.

There is one quirky thing about French men and sex, and it is this: they're completely and utterly obsessed with the bottom. Or, as the French like to refer to it, *le cul.*

I remember the first time a French man said to me, *'Oh, quel cul t'as!'* ('Oh, what an arse you have!') It was in a bar and it shocked and disturbed me so much I couldn't summon up a reply. (And not just because my *derrière* is so generous it could ask for its own passport.) *'Magnifique!'* he kept repeating, surveying the rear of my new French jeans like an architect analysing a Frank Gehry curve. *'Magnifique!'* I didn't know what to say. We hadn't even reached the heavy groping stage and he was marking me like an art class. After a few minutes of wince-inducing *magnifiques*, I became so unsettled I politely ended the conversation and went in search of a stiff *pastis*.

Days later, while watching Parisian women rush past from my seat at a café on St-Sulpice, I had an epiphany. The majority of French females don't have bottoms. It's just not fashionable. Balenciaga doesn't design for big butts. In place of backsides they have flat, firm, hard things. *Derrières* you could serve a cognac off. And so any woman who displays something remotely resembling a soft, plump behind—and there are some out there—are immediately worshipped by a certain percentage of French men. It's obviously sometimes nicer to fondle flesh than a bony behind. Even though I still think the latter looks better in size eight jeans.

(Napoleon apparently loved Josephine's bum so much he declared it was the best thing he'd ever seen. Although it had to be better than her teeth, which at the time of their marriage reportedly resembled black cloves. For her part though, Josephine put up with just as much imperfection in her husband. It is said that Napoleon suffered from scabies and his face was a hazard of foul-smelling sores. He also had a small penis, allegedly. If you're curious, one inch is the suggested length, according to those he slept with.)

Fascinated by this unexpected side to French sex and seduction, I decided to go back to the same bar the next night and ask my buttock-obsessed friend, who was called Eric, why the sight of two cheeks set off his libido so. He replied that it was the one part of the body that was still a mystery. Breasts, he said, were everywhere, and even the lower front of a woman—he grabbed his crotch—was tossed about the media like nobody's business. But a bum—ah, the humble bum, he said fondly—was still sacred. And what a good thing it was too.

'It is the cause of *le plaisir*,' he purred.

So then, I replied, should I stop with my no-French-food diet and just enjoy my behind?

To which he removed his cigarette, exhaled slowly and made a clucking sound of disapproval. '*Les anglais.* You are worse than Parisians. Your arse is a fine thing,' he said, getting ready to screw his cigarette back in. 'Never forget that. It is a treasure to be loved.'

I went home, looked at my behind in the mirror, and tried to make peace with my padded backside. It almost worked.

After a few weeks of discussing *le cul* with Eric whenever I went to this bistro for a drink, I found I began to like my new French friend more and more. Well, who wouldn't? A man in touch with a woman's arse is a man to love, in my opinion. In fact, it was probably because of this that he was the first Frenchman I found *séduisant*—appealing—even though he looked slightly like a squashed Jerusalem artichoke that's fallen off the back of a vegetable cart. Pretty soon, I began to fall for my buttock-obsessed friend. Unfortunately, however, Eric was busy falling for someone else. A Swedish sous chef named Ulrika, whom he had met under the vaulted cellar of a basement jazz club one night.

It was bad timing. All I heard for the next few weeks were odes to the lovely Ulrika. How Ulrika could do wonders with a saucisson and manipulate *les carottes, les courgettes* and *les aubergines* at the same time.

'*Ooh la la*,' he murmured, shaking his head. '*Mon dieu, mon dieu.*'

I never knew whether he was referring to her kitchen skills or some other skill she practised with her tongue.

After a while, it began to disturb me. I mean, how on earth was an

Australian girl to compete with a Swedish goddess—particularly one able to perform several sexual and culinary feats at once?

One day, Eric was in mid-oration about the orifices of the Swedish bombshell—having stayed in her apartment for three days straight without, apparently, emerging once for air—when I decided I'd had enough.

'Stop!' I said, holding up my hand. 'Ulrika is coming between us. In more ways than one.'

'Pardon?' said Eric, startled out of his Ulrika-induced reverie.

'Look, I like you, but I don't want to hear what you can do with your tongue and the bits of Ulrika that don't see the sun!'

My new friend tried hard not to look surprised. But then he got all huffy and went off, no doubt to explore Ulrika a little bit more. Honestly. You would have thought the girl was a topographical map, the way he pored over her contours.

I felt slightly hurt by Eric and his obsession with Swedish bits and so I emailed a girlfriend of mine in Australia to ponder the problem via broadband. She emailed back in *tsk tsk* tones. 'Janelle,' she wrote, in a way that made me feel she was shaking her head as she did so. 'You've got to understand that there is a division between the girls French men want to sleep with and the girls they want to marry. We, you and me, we are the girls they may want to eventually marry. But until that day comes, Ulrika has the floor.'

'Why?' I wrote back, perplexed.

'It's our schooling,' she said simply.

Now Kate and I attended the same school. But I couldn't understand the connection between it and the reluctance of French men like Eric to have sex with us.

'It's the private school factor,' she went on, knowing a little about French men from four years of roaming Europe. 'It's because we attended a girls' school.'

I stared at the computer screen, hoping I wasn't going to read what

I was about to read. 'Private school girls spend six years being sheltered from boys, you see, so by the time they emerge from their ladylike domain they're about the horniest little people you've ever going to meet.' (This was true: I knew of many uptight, beautifully mannered daughters of millionaires who went on to university and were so shocked at the availability of ready testosterone, they proceeded to sleep with everything in sight.)

'The thing is,' she continued, 'private school girls have been so sheltered, they're not like normal girls. They're, well, stuck in this ladylike mould they can't break free from. And men recognise this. They love the fact that we've spent so long learning how to be a lady we now just want to be treated like a callgirl. But when it comes to treating us like one, they just can't get past our upbringing. Talking dirty with a private school girl is a little like doing the business with a nun. It's just not possible. So you see, my dear friend, the private school curse is upon you. But I wish you all the best of luck!'

What a load of myth and *merde*, I thought, frowning and turning off the computer. There had to be a way to lift the curse. I had kissed my share of boys and not one of them had ever asked where I had been educated. I had to prove it was a fallacy. I had to prove that well-brought-up Australian girls were just as good as the French *petites filles* at dipping an eyelash and cooing like Lauren Bacall.

So I rang an ex-boyfriend in London, Blair, whose mother was French and grandfather was Italian (which technically made him two-thirds Latin). I remembered that he had emailed me about coming to Paris on business at some stage, and I suddenly thought that it might be nice to catch up. After all, there's nothing like a bit of a booty call to lift a girl's spirits.

'Bonjour, Ms McCulloch! To what do I owe the pleasure of this call?'

And so I explained the situation: that I wanted to meet for dinner when he was in town, followed by some dancing if he fancied it, and then, I added in suggestive tones, well who knew where the Seine would take us?

'Oh, *ma chère*,' he said in a mock French accent.

I found out when he was arriving, and then gave him an address. At the last minute I added that I'd meet him there. It wasn't a date, after all. Just a booty call.

I spent all of the next day getting ready. And possibly some of the day before. I hadn't had an eyebrow wax let alone a bikini one in months and needed maintenance desperately. I deliberated over spending an insane amount of money on highlights but then decided I couldn't afford it on a freelancer's salary and so wore my hair up, trailing a few what I hoped were flirtatious wisps, glued down with spray. I spritzed Guerlain's L'Heure Bleue liberally into the air and then stepped into it, as my French friends had taught me to do, and then screwdrivered myself into a new red corset and a red and white silk wrap skirt that screamed Parisian hedonism at ten paces. As my friend Holly would have said, it was 'sex with a hemline on it'. Private school or not, I thought, here I come.

Now a pair of strappy black heels will do wonders for a girl's morale but a drop-dead sexy outfit will do things only imagined in fantasies. When I stepped out of the taxi and walked across the street to the front of the restaurant Blair looked like you could have knocked him over with a kitten heel. He approached me quietly and gave me a gentle kiss on both cheeks that spoke not only of *tendresse* but the sexual tension that comes with the expectation of great things. One part of me was quietly thrilled. The other was praying I didn't resemble a cheap *salonnière* (courtesan).

Sensing my discomfort, he immediately took charge, opening the restaurant's front door for us and putting his hand on the small of my back as we passed through. The gesture was astonishingly sexy. I have always wanted someone to do this—put his hand there—and now it was happening. The French call it *attentionné*, when a man guides you like this. *Attentionné.* Just the word sounded romantic. We were, I noted silently to myself, officially entering fantasyland. Blair announced us to the maître d' and we took our seats. It was then I could see what I was letting myself in for. And it wasn't bad. My fake date was wearing a dark Dunhill suit—the kind of classic black number that makes any man look like a British contender for the next James Bond—and a crisp white shirt with silver Tiffany cufflinks. He looked roguish but literate. And utterly irresistible.

I felt the butterflies in my stomach, and thought of the seventeenth-century salon hostesses who often received friends in their bedrooms. If they could do it with such brazen openness, I thought, so could I.

I wondered what to do first: get drunk, or get drunk. And then, just as I was about to decide to do both, my arms started to break apart, exploding into great huge red welts that looked like I'd just emerged from hacking through the Congo.

Blair looked understandably alarmed. The prospect of sex was fading before his eyes as the rash grew larger and larger in mine. I couldn't imagine what it was. A heat rash? A nervous reaction? Or just an odd aversion to a bit of impromptu booty? Yes. It was an allergic reaction to unadulterated sex. I was certain of it. I'd never done a booty call before and my body was warning me of the consequences.

Blair decided, perhaps sensibly, that the night wasn't about to unfold as planned, and led me outside to find a taxi. Embarrassed, I told him not to worry, and I think he was secretly relieved. Perhaps he thought I'd caught some weird French disease from a scoundrel like Eric and he didn't relish the prospect of flying home with a whole lot of anti-inflammatories filling his bag.

As he walked off—a little faster than normal, I noticed—I went straight to the pharmacie and brandished my arms at the white-coated man, speaking French nonsense in pidgin fashion.

'*Excusez-moi de vous déranger, monsieur, mais j'ai un problème!*' I said, crying and waving my arms like a madwoman. '*Regardez! Peau! Peau!*'

I added, pointing at my pink arms and repeating the word for skin as if it was going to clarify the problem.

Silently, and (I sensed) a little warily, the chemist reached to a far shelf and handed me a box of something that looked suspiciously like wart remover. Or herbal tablets for some obscure venereal disease. In any case it had an appalling, badly photographed image on the cover that looked like a modern manifestation of the bubonic plague.

The lady beside me, who was replenishing her supply of moisturiser, moved sideways, as if to remove herself from my whore-ific life. I quietly paid the chemist for whatever the box was, said *merci* with a meek squeak, and moved discreetly back outside.

I walked home, threw the box in the bin, ran a cool bath with tears in my eyes and didn't move for an hour until the rash went down.

And that was the end of my French-style sex.

Understanding the French

Boy, those French. They have a different word
for everything.

Steve Martin

It is *la rentrée* in Paris as I write this, and all around me in my little neighbourhood a new year is beginning. *La rentrée*, which literally means 'reentry', is a particular Parisian syndrome and one that I have come to observe with growing curiosity.

The word, a fabulous description if ever I've heard one, refers to that frenzied time of year when Parisians return to town after their summer sojourns and the city stretches and repositions itself, in an urban version of yoga, to mentally and physically ready itself for the metropolitan onslaught. All through late August and early September there is a kind of gusto as traffic refills the streets, people unpack their bags, children return to school, and the rest reacquaint themselves with their *boulanger* and fishmonger to catch up on the neighbourhood gossip.

Basically, *la rentrée* is when routine resumes with a quiet new solemnity. Even though much of the city is *stressé* and *pressé*—stressed and in a hurry.

In the Odéon quarter, *la rentrée* is still in full swing, even though we are now well into September. The wealthy denizens of the sixth and seventh can afford to spend an extra week or two at their summer cottages and stone farmhouses in the country, although those with pressing work deadlines returned some weeks ago; their skin still pink from a frantic few weeks in the sun and their Bensimon sandshoes still poignantly grasping grains of sand. The rest are drifting back now, with their cars full of holiday clothes and obscure wine bought from strange cellar doors after they took a detour and got lost, via Alsace, on the way home.

As the *quartier* slowly returns to normality after the ebbs and flows of a summer that hasn't seemed long enough, thoughts are turning to deadlines, to diaries and social functions, and to new season's wardrobes. Life is moving swiftly into a new gear. A new year has begun.

There is a wistfulness to Paris in the months of September and October as Parisians sigh over the inevitable end of summer and the fading summer light, pull on their cardigans and coats, and head resignedly into autumn. Much of the capital spends September trying to come to terms with the loss of another summer, and many of the bars, bistros, grassy knolls and café terraces are jammed with people at once embracing and mourning the lingering sun. In the boulevards of my *quartier* there is a explosion of frantic *flâneurs* as workers use their lunch hours to pace the avenues and plan their wardrobes/parties/weekends, while others take the day off and sit and reflect on a terrace for the prolonged period between brunch and *l'apéro*.

Several of my neighbours, judging by the silence of their apartments, are still out of town, and those who have returned seem to spend much of their time indulging in overpriced brunches with friends. I've spotted them now and then when I pop out for supplies, smiling to myself as I hear them compare notes on holiday homes and the escalating price of oysters on the coast.

I would tell you more about what they're saying but my French learning curve has plateaued out of late and my speaking skills have reached a conversational cul-de-sac. I thought I might be better by now, I thought I would have learned more, even by osmosis, but I must have picked up the wrong language book from the travel bookstore by mistake. So far all I have learned are the major fashion labels, a few basics—*d'accord*; *je ne comprends pas*; *parlez plus lentement s'il vous plaît* (please speak more slowly); and Greta Garbo's favourite, *je veux être seule* (I'd like to be alone)—which doesn't really get me far on a social level. Of course, I know some other phrases, which are not overly helpful but are nonetheless intriguing: *Où peut-on trouver un peu d'air?* (Where do I find some fresh air?); *J'ai enfermé mon bébé dans l'armoire* (I have locked my baby in the cupboard); and *C'est vraiment du thé, ça?* (Is this really tea?). I try to use them whenever I can, just to practise my accent.

There's another saying that I particularly like, which goes like this: *Pourrais-je laisser mon mari avec le concierge?* I think it translates as 'May I please leave my husband with the concierge?' I don't know when I'd ever use it. Which is a pity, really, because I think it's rather grand.

But perhaps the best French phrase that I've learned of late is *faire une connerie*, which literally means 'to fuck up' (if you'll excuse my French). Of course, I didn't know it meant 'to fuck up' until some kind person—Alexandra, I think—pointed it out to me. Until that stage I had simply assumed it meant 'to make a mistake', and had been using it all over town, including at several smart luncheons. I can only look back in horror at what all the Frenchwomen thought. And understand why I haven't been invited back to those luncheons again.

Before I came to Paris the only French words I could remember from university tutorials—and a separate but far more rewarding education via the cosmetics and fashion departments of David Jones—were Crème de la Mer, Chanel *Précision Lift Sérum Extrême* and Yves Saint Laurent *Touche Éclat*. Over the years and visits I picked up bits and pieces that were slightly more relevant to modern life, like *salut, bonjour* and *le vin*. I never quite adopted the French of my favourite waiter at Melbourne's France Soir restaurant, with his endearing glottal slurs, but I thought I was doing okay.

That is, until I stayed here longer than a week. The French not only speak much faster than any university lecturer or cosmetics representative, they do it with finesse. So words you think you might have known suddenly change shape, twist into an accent and fly out of the mouths of those speaking them with such rapid-fire rat-a-tat-tat delivery that trying to catch them is like trying to catch a speeding bullet and read its origins on the way past. I've given up trying to carry on an articulate conversation. Now, in order not to look like a complete idiot, I pause and nod a lot, as if to agree with everything my new French friends are saying.

To make matters worse, I keep getting the words that I have learned mixed up with the slang ones that I haven't quite learned. At a cocktail party a few weeks ago I kept referring to *le sexe*, arguing that if French men can have mistresses, why can't French women? It was only during the lull between conversations that my hostess gently pointed out that *le sexe* refers to the male appendage, not the English word for sex, and that I had just spent the last half-hour raving about penises.

I barely survived the evening with my *dignité* intact. All I knew, when I left feeling slightly *de trop*, was that my language skills were not only going from *de mal en pis* (bad to worse), but *de pis en pis*. From awful to positively *merde*.

I'm sure it's difficult for anyone trying to converse in a strange tongue, but for journalists it's particularly wrenching. Most of us articulate for a living. So to come to France and suddenly be unable to converse or even come up with *le mot juste*—the right word—is like losing a leg for an athlete or a tongue for a tenor. You feel foolish. Ignorant. And worst of all, illiterate. It's terrible. Especially when you live in a *quartier* famous for its *intellos*. I can only imagine they walk away shaking their heads saying, '*Espèce d'andouille!*' (which roughly translates as 'What an illiterate idiot!').

I console myself with the thought that many other people have come to France not speaking a word of the language and somehow survived and lived to order another cup of *café noir*. Surely they progressed from pitiful pidgin French to a perfect accent; from croissant and Chanel to dinner party debates about the state of politics? The language can't be that hard to master. Give me another drink and I'm sure I can do more than mime.

If the grammar wasn't enough for a visitor to contend with, however, there is also a whole new set of social codes to memorise. And they're not the kind you learn from your *Petit Larousse* dictionary.

The most perplexing of all these codes, I have discovered, is the unwritten rule that says you must not reply in the affirmative to anyone during your first year here. Parisians see it as a sign of weakness. Personally, I can't imagine how you can go for an entire year without saying yes. I mean, what if a fruiterer asked if you wanted some of the new season's apples with your purchase of pears? Or a barman asked if you wanted more gin with your tonic? Were you to say *non* to everything, just to satisfy some silly Parisian social code? I can't imagine what would happen if someone gorgeous Frenchman asked you out for a drink.

I love Paris, but sometimes the city can seem very strange.

It's especially difficult for an Australian to adhere to these new rules because we tend to say yes to everything on offer: yes to more beer or wine at backyard barbecues; yes to more lemon with our salt and pepper calamari; and yes to more money when the mortgage lender offers to bury us up to our necks in debt. And we certainly say yes when good-looking people come up to us in glamorous bars and offer to buy us a drink. (Australian girls are not that stupid. We'll take the champagne, thanks very much, and run.)

So to come to France and be faced with a social code that discourages any kind of affirmative reply is particularly challenging. Especially when a dark-haired stranger approaches me on the street and says '*Voulez-vous venir avec moi dans un café?*', which I think translates, as 'Would you like to come for a coffee with me?' Although with my pitiful French I could be very wrong. And then saying yes might turn out to be very awkward indeed.

It is mid-morning and, while *la rentrée* continues to swirl around in the streets outside, I have spent the best part of three hours on the internet trying to research the city. And the language these citizens speak.

It is in the middle of all this Googling—typing 'French' and 'easy' and 'achieving fluency in ten breezy steps' that I stumble over a website with odd instructions on *être*—how to 'be' when you live in France. Beautiful, I think. Just what I need.

First of all (it says), you need to understand the art of *engueuler* (or dressing people down). This is imperative if you want to get anything done in France, particularly with *petits bureaucrates* or anyone with the smallest airs or graces, even if they only work in a *chocolatier.*

Intrigued, I read on.

To be taken seriously, particularly in Paris, you have to know how to *râler, gronder, et enguirlander*. In other words, stand up straight, look people in the eye and stand your ground. In France, confrontation is the only way, this site says, to get things done.

Oh no, I think, reading it with growing horror. I have to get tough with the descendants of the Revolutionaries and the maker of the guillotine?

Now I am perfectly capable of reprimanding someone when the situation calls for it. My father is a retired school principal, so I learned a few tricks from him. When I was a magazine editor, I went from being someone sweet and kind who said sorry even when it wasn't my fault to a virtual 'ball breaker', almost overnight. (The job requires it, believe me.) One of my photographers told me I was such a ball breaker, he always felt his manly bits shrivel up, clang to the ground and roll out the door whenever I opened my mouth. (An exaggeration, I hope.) Now that those days are over, however, I no longer switch to 'ruthless' mode unless I'm dealing with a telco about a phone connection. My father would be horrified if he thought I raised my voice just to win an argument.

So the idea of adopting *engueuler* feels wrong somehow, even if it does, apparently, make life in the French capital much easier to bear.

I don't realise my first lesson in *engueuler* is about to begin.

An hour or so later, just as I'm getting ready to go out and have a *thé à la rose* and a little plate of *millefeuille* and macaroons at Ladurée, there is a knock on the door. It is Sophie, my neighbour, who's married to a man who works in finance (or something). Sophie often seems bored when I pass her on rue St-Sulpice, and occasionally I wonder if the job of a banker's wife isn't stimulating enough for a woman who, with her dark bob, looks like she ought to be in the Moulin Rouge. Sometimes I feel like tapping her on the arm and saying 'Hi' in that informal Australian fashion (complete with a smile, even though it's apparently banned here), and asking if she wants to go for a coffee. But French *politesse* prevents me and we simply pass and nod on the street.

At least, I think we nod. It's so imperceptible, it could merely be that she's looking from me down to the dog *merde* on the pavement.

I often wondered why neighbours who live beside each other for decades rarely say hello, if ever, and then one day I read an article by a journalist who discovered, under the heading 'Étiquette' in an old Larousse encyclopedia, that, according to French custom, when two people pass in the street it is up to the 'inferior' person to say hello first. French people, however, don't like feeling inferior, or indeed being inferior, and so the modern tradition of ignoring your neighbour lives on.

One day Sophie did say '*Bonjour*' to me quite suddenly and I brightened, thinking it was the start of a new friendship. But then someone behind me said '*Bonjour*' back and I realised she was speaking to the interior decorator from the third floor.

But now—wonders of wonders—here she is, at my door, asking, from what I can make out, if I want to come for dinner. '*Bonjour*, madame. I, er—we—live upstairs. My name is Sophie. Um, we would like to invite you to *dîner*,' she says, looking ever so slightly uncomfortable. And then, perhaps to shorten the whole awkward, awful procedure of speaking to the gauche Australian neighbour, she hands me a little card—a *pour mémoire*—outlining all the details: dress code, time, even the menu (to understand which, I would need Gordon Ramsay to translate).

I feel a little thrill of excitement. '*Merci*,' I say, trying not to sound too happy. 'I would love to come, and meet your, er—' I don't know what to add here—'charming husband.'

'*Bon*,' she says warily, looking at me as if I'm about to shag her man and eying off the *mémoire* card as if she should perhaps grab it back. '*Bon!* Ah, goodnight, then.'

And the embarrassing transaction is complete.

To be asked to dinner in Paris is the ultimate invitation. You do not turn it down. It is harder to get into a French dinner party than

Brad Pitt's pants. It is twice as hard if you are English. (Australians fall into this league.) To put it bluntly, the French don't like English company. At least, not at their dinner tables: the high altar of French living. To swig a glass of Bordeaux alongside *les anglais* at, say, Ascot, or some swish new restaurant in the West End, is all very well, but when it comes to their own turf, they'd much rather the English go and do their tasteless, vulgar style of living elsewhere.

Even the French outposts don't like us. I've been on holiday in Tahiti and the local grocery store owner all but grimaced at my Anglicised French. 'Do not bother yourself, madame, it's quite okay,' he growled, shooing me with an urgent wave out of his chic little store.

Such is their attitude towards us that *à l'anglaise* in French refers to the way the English (supposedly) behave; the overt manner in which they speak (in that dreadful English way) and the, well, English things they do. In short, English are *sans gêne*: uncouth and without embarrassment. The French have even coined phrases for our terrible dinner party behaviour: *filer à l'anglaise*, which means to leave a room 'English-style', without saying *bonne nuit* or *merci beaucoup* for the pig's ears and the *tête de veau*.

Yes, indeed, there's no love lost between the French and the English, let alone an understanding between the nations. Forget that words like *beau*, in the sense of 'dandy' or 'suitor', actually came from England (extrapolated from the famous Englishman, Beau Brummell). The French, for the most part, feel that it is much better if the English stay firmly on that side of the Channel.

So I am naturally nervous when the night of the dinner party swings around. I want to write down lots of little French phrases on the back of my wrist, like a French exam, to refer to when the going gets tough. But somehow I don't think that will be appreciated. And besides, I'd have to squint to understand the tiny type. And the other guests might think I was having a *petit mal*, a seizure.

It was *le Roi Soleil*, the great Sun King, who introduced the French dinner party as we know it today. He called this kind of service *à la française* and almost immediately the elaborate style of dining became recognised as the grandest form of entertaining. It became the international byword (or byphrase) for having a good time.

A true dinner *à la française* is a feast fit for a king, although it also has overtones of Peter Greenaway's film *The Cook, The Thief, His Wife and Her Lover* about it. Everyone seems rather ready for death by digestion. I've heard of some French dinner parties that last for days, with guests dropping like legless flies around the table.

A typical dinner *à la française* includes almost as many courses as a *dégustation* menu. There's the *potage*, followed by the *hors-d'oeuvre* (*crudités, charcuterie, pâtés* or *quiche*), the *entrée* (cold or hot), the main course, or *le plat principal*, and then the *plateau de fromages* (the cheese plate) and, finally, the *entremets* (fruit, sorbets, cakes, compotes, whatever else you can fit in) and a *pousse-café*. To aid digestion, which is obviously necessary, the hostess will usually also serve a triple sec and a *tisane*.

I wonder if I should also bring some good old Alka-Seltzer in a little whisky flask, just to be sure.

When the night arrives I am so anxious (I haven't eaten for two days in preparation for it) that a little pre-dinner drink goes straight to my head. I am *pompette* before the dinner party has even begun. The invitation has suggested 'Carnivale' for the dress code, which I naturally interpret, in French (and also magazine editor-style) fashion, as 'black'. I have worn a demure black dress and fashioned my hair into what I hope is an acceptable chignon. When I arrive, however, all the others present bar one—the waiter—are wearing bright shades. Next to them, I look like a nun. I feel *déclassée* from the start.

Sophie makes the introductions and I shake hands with each. They are all our neighbours but I can't for the life of me remember anyone's names and so, like the French version of *Reservoir Dogs*, give them all quirky noms de plume: Monsieur *Pink*, Madame *Cerise*; Mademoiselle *Framboise*. I hope the evening doesn't draw on too long or I may end up calling someone Monsieur *Vert* by mistake.

The most important things you have to learn, when you start mixing with the French, are a) the art of lively conversation, and b) the art of *bien élevé*, or being well mannered. Nothing else matters at French dinner parties: not your social status or your clothes labels or what university you've gone to or even which celebrity you've recently slept with. You could be a Rhodes scholar and you'd still be ostracised if you don't have something witty to say.

There are other things you should learn, too, like not bringing wine unless agreed ahead of time with the host. Bringing some dodgy bottle of plonk you picked up at a bin sale will simply insult your host and imply that any old label will go with the undistinguished fare he or she is about to serve.

It also pays to empty your bladder before you arrive, because asking to use the 'little room' is akin to asking to take a little catnap in the master boudoir—with your hostess's husband for company. (Some guests, according to a fabulous guide I've found called *French or Foe*, will even stop the car and take a pee in the bushes before they arrive, in anticipation of not being allowed to leave their seats for four hours straight.) Apparently it's considered an unforgivable felony to excuse oneself to go to the bathroom during dinner at a restaurant or private home. Bladder diplomacy, it seems, is a big issue at French dinner tables.

And then there is the order of procedure, which only begins once everyone has arrived. You will not be given a drink until the very last person has passed through the door so don't help yourself to the *Brut rosé* while you're waiting for the evening to start.

You will also most likely be seated on soft, low-slung chairs—the kind that Christian Liaigre has made famous—for an hour or more before the meal begins, so watch your alcohol intake during that time or you'll have trouble extricating yourself from the cushion. And will most likely fall headfirst into your neighbour's lap.

When you do eventually stumble drunkenly to your feet, watch who passes through the door to the dining room first, because it will not be you. French protocol dictates that the highest-ranked guest gets to walk through first, so unless you're royalty, aristocratic, from the government or a person of the church, hang back and let the others slide on in.

Once seated, keep your hands at table level. Good manners decree that hands should be *on* the table at *all* times. The French feel funny seeing Anglo-Saxons (who have been raised the opposite way) keeping their fingers close to their laps; they worry that unmentionable things are being done while the wine is being poured.

I once heard the story of an American man who was confronted by his French host after the latter spotted the former resting his hands in his lap between courses.

'What are you doing with your hand, playing with yourself?' barked the Frenchman, only half in jest.

'No, actually I'm playing with your wife!' retorted the American.

Most of the dinner table laughed. The Frenchman did not. And the American never came to dinner again.

At some stage during the dinner party proceedings, you may be offered a drink, and quite often it will be champagne. You need to take it. It's rude not to. Even if you're already feeling *pompette* from all those kir royals. The host or hostess will continue to offer you alcohol during the meal, and it is good manners to accept this too. But don't even *think* about visiting the little men's or ladies' room. Because you're not leaving the table until every last bottle is empty. And that includes the port.

Whatever you do, don't turn up late, or too early; serve yourself more wine (even if you feel you need it to survive the night); consider the labels of what you're drinking, as if it's not up to standard; or leave before midnight. Most of all, don't show up with an uninvited guest, even if he is someone you've spent the entire afternoon having passionate sex with. The hostess has gone to an enormous amount of trouble to seat people in convivial groups: an extra person will throw out her delicate order. And you'll never be invited over again.

I think I know most of this before I front up to Sophie's, thanks to the instructions of *French or Foe*, and, apart from the stomach full of *kirs*, feel comfortable about the night ahead. I don't realise that none of the guests have previously met. And the night is about to come to a crashing standstill.

'The Frenchman,' Henry Miller wrote, 'protects the vessel which contains the spirit.' He was referring to the famous French reserve, which kicks into place when the French are unsure of a social situation, or haven't dealt with each other for, say, more than two years. It's called *ils se défendent*: defending yourself against the unknown. And it can have dire consequences if everyone is doing it.

At eight pm, when all the guests have filtered into the salon and Sophie leaves to uncork the champagne, we all find, with unease, that we have no history together, other than sharing an apartment building, and therefore nothing to say. The silence is excruciating.

'Are you a writer?' says the man from the top floor, trying to break down the walls.

'Yes, *une journaliste*,' I reply.

'Oh?' he says, and the conversation ends there.

I begin to feel the familiar rash that always comes when you're dropped somewhere without a proper map. Strange places like Parisian dinner parties can be hazardous, full of potholes of faux pas. I take another gulp of my wine, not caring that I'm already well on the way to being calmly intoxicated.

I try to chat to a strange lady who speaks in exclamation marks, and whose collagen-injected lips are so large they could have declared themselves an independent state. But before I've said *bonjour* she's drifted away to another corner. I desperately need the toilet, but I can't remember which door led back to the hall.

A small blonde with a large cleavage attached offers me *hors d'oeuvre* from an oversized platter. 'We're having a *mélange* tonight instead of *haricots verts*,' she says quietly in a heavy French accent. 'Apparently it's the new thing.'

I nod politely and fill my plate, not knowing what to say. The rest of the guests simply stand there, studying the parquetry floor.

Sophie returns and seats us in a complicated arrangement that involves lots of shuffling and manoeuvring of feet. It's like musical chairs without the music.

For several hours I am lost in translation while the conversation touches on French architecture, actors, a few jokes I don't understand and a debate about bread. Eventually, a gentleman looks my way.

'So, you are from Australia?' says the professorial-looking man dressed in an odd yellowish shade of lime green—*vert tilleul*, I think it's called—as the main course of *rillettes de saumon* is served.

'Yes, Melbourne actually,' I reply. 'Do you know it?'

'No,' he says. 'But I am very interested in the Outback. And the Aborigines. How is it that the Australian government can address such a significant issue with so little gravitas?'

Now I am not ready for a debate about cultures. It is a difficult conversation to have when you're stone-cold sober, let alone slightly sozzled, and is also one that's best left to a situation where you are all speaking the same language.

'The Aboriginal issue is very, er, tragic, and also very complicated,' I say, fumbling for words. 'They receive a great deal of funding from the Australian government, a *great* deal, and are also regularly given tracts of land—vast tracts of land: Uluru, or Ayers Rock, is effectively theirs and you have to ask permission to enter the site. But no amount of money will compensate for a century of ill treatment from the whites, and the destruction of a culture that was once so great. I can see how the government finds it hard to know what to do. On one side is the modern world, with its modern economy and customs, in which everyone is expected to participate, even those immigrants who land straight off the plane from overseas; on the other side, a dignified Aboriginal history that is so much a part of Australia's own story. It is very hard—for everyone. The right solutions are still being found.'

I look around the table. Some look interested; others grim. I don't know if I've ventured into a minefield, or if current affairs are a forbidden topic. And then I remember: keep the conversation light. Nobody wants to partake in a debate about cross-cultural issues. We could do that here at the dinner table—between the French and English—if that was the case.

I feel as if I've just completed a colossal faux pas.

'Yes, well,' laughs the same gentleman. 'I suppose we cannot expect much from a country built from convicts, really, can we?'

I am incensed. I have just tried to explain, as sensitively and as diplomatically as I can, an issue which crosses not only decades but also cultures, races and governments, and here is some old *blagueur* putting the problem down to a bunch of prisoners from England. I can't help it. I snap.

'Monsieur Vert,' I say with fierce *engueuler*. 'This is not an issue you will readily understand.' And then I lose it, well and truly, to the point where I mix my insults with my slang. 'In fact, how dare you! That is an *andouille* thing to say!'

I can't go on. I have just accused him of being a sausage. There is nothing more to say.

Thankfully Sophie breaks the ice with an interjection about *la rentrée* and we are left to retire, sore and tender, to our separate corners.

The next day, recovering from a head that feels like a squashed lemon and a feeling that I've gone too far with my *engueuler*, and will no longer have any friends left in the entire street and perhaps even the city, I venture outside to find a cup of tea. Preferably with lots of liquor in it.

As I step tentatively down the stairs, Monsieur Vert strolls into the courtyard, carrying his papers and a parcel from Poilâne.

'*Bonjour, madame!*' he says brightly, giving me a little wave. 'How are we today?'

I am astonished. *Astonished.* '*Bonjour, monsieur,*' I reply tentatively. '*Bien. Et vous?*'

'Fine. Just fine,' he winks, with a dandyesque wiggle. 'No *andouille* today?' And then he continues on up the stairs, chuckling to himself.

The French. Honestly. I love them to bits, but I don't think I'll ever understand them.

. 8 .

L'Art de Vivre

THE ART OF LIVING

The heart of Paris is like nothing so much as the unending interior of a house. Buildings become furniture, courtyards become carpets and arrases, the streets are like galleries, the boulevards conservatories. It is a house, one or two centuries old, rich, bourgeois, distinguished.

John Berger

Last week the weather turned. It happened when everyone was preoccupied with something else—sex and food and drinking, no doubt—and saturated the city in gloomy spirits. In the parks, which now seem melancholy without the summer frivolity, the leaves have suddenly turned brown underfoot and now remain there, sad and sodden in the rain. The Seine, I noticed yesterday when I popped out for an amble with an umbrella for company, has lost its beautiful diamond lustre and now just looks like a chain of cheap cubic zirconia copies draped around the Île St-Louis. The skies, which are normally a soft shade of oyster grey, are now a moody, brooding black.

The sudden winter nip in the air has made everyone reach hurriedly for their jackets and scarves, watching with forlorn regret as café chairs disappear from terraces and market umbrellas snap shut, to be put away for another day. Everywhere you look there is a general air of despondency about the streets. Autumn, it seems, has settled in for good.

But the turning of the seasons has had an upside in that city chefs, the constant barometers of Paris's changing seasons, are rolling up their sleeves with new-season enthusiasm and changing menus to embrace more hearty winter dishes—like sautéed wild mushrooms and rabbits in mustard sauce. As a result, cafés are filling with bright lights and an inviting gaiety. People are settling in and ordering *coq au vin* and an extra bottle of Bordeaux. The seasons may be changing but life in Paris is becoming a whole lot more promising.

Autumn and winter are the best times to linger in Parisian bars and cafés. The condensation on the windows makes them feel cosier, somehow, and there are quiet pleasures to be had in seeing others rush past outside. I love to linger in Parisian bistros, bars and cafés, soaking up the atmosphere and the chat. It makes you feel as though you really are a part, albeit a small one, of Parisian society.

It also makes you realise the significance to the French of their interior spaces—the public ones as much as the private ones—and the unerring sense of taste they have obviously inherited from centuries of stylish living. For the French, an interior is not just a place to go when the weather is inclement: it is a space to create a feeling of warmth, style, comfort and complete sophistication.

To get an idea of how the French interior is fast becoming the epitome of design chic, next time you're roaming around Paris, visit the exquisitely tiny Hôtel Le A in the heart of the highly elegant eighth.

Now the lovely people at the A, as you can gather from the name, don't like to overdo things. That would be too, well, *dépassé*. They believe that harmony lies in subtlety and, for that reason, commissioned the maestro of monochromatic sophistication, Frédéric Méchiche, to design the A's fiercely chic interior. The result is pure poetic simplicity—a space that doesn't so much shriek glamour as murmurs it in suggestive tones. The reception area and library are a dramatic slash of black while the bar is a whisper of white. Upstairs in the suites, which are also decked out in the fashion set's favourite shades, the bedrooms and ensuites are an irresistible swish of marle grey and white, and so seductive you wish you had a well-dressed lover to share them with.

Beloved by models, stylists, photographers and magazine editors, particularly during fashion weeks, it is a perfect slice of *l'élégance française*. To use a well-worn cliché, the A is *ooh là là*.

On the other side of the city, in the quietly gracious sixteenth, is the Trocadéro Dokhan's Hotel, another Frédéric Méchiche-designed bolthole, though one that caters for a similarly well-dressed but slightly different business set: one that likes things a little more 'buttoned up' and less fluid and free. Here, Méchiche has created an interior that shimmers with class, although there's still a little Parisian whimsy in the mix. (One journalist called the style 'early Neoclassical *bonbonnière*'.) The hall is decked out in bold black and white awning stripes; the elevator is covered in panels from an antique Louis Vuitton trunk; the chequerboard marble floor compels you to don your most beautifully polished shoes even when you're simply checking in; and the ecru curtains are sewn with the care of an *haute couture* gown.

Downstairs, the city's only champagne bar is a haven of bubbly-inspired delight, offering foie gras, caviar and salmon to wash down your pick of perfect brut vintages.

With its careful mix of balance and harmony, romance and beauty, it is the equivalent of a candy shop for adults. And it's been whipping Left Bank *intellos* into a design-led frenzy for years. As one friend says, 'it's porn for creative professionals'.

Oh, the *chic* of it!

Yet despite their fascination with perfection and form, Parisians have a curious fondness for odd bits and pieces, and tend to cater to this love of *folie* by collecting things in spades. And buckets. And trucks. Every French person I know has this little foible: they embrace clutter—and the more of it the better. Books, bric-a-brac, porcelain plates, taxidermied animals: any kind of flea market find usually makes the grade. Why do you think the stallholders of the city's antique markets are so quietly rich?

In order to style all this mismatching clutter, Parisians have to rely on the rules and disciplines of design. Symmetry is one secret; arranging things in sympathetic vignettes is another. Some, however, just forget all that and shove the stuff wherever it fits, leading to apartments that look less like cosy homes than fearsome curiosity shops.

But there is a collective change in decorative taste taking place. Beguiled by the new lines practised by the likes Méchiche and Christian Liaigre, a man for whom honesty of form equals elegance of space, Parisians are slowly adopting a new design paradigm—one that's ruled by uncompromising simplicity. And I mean uncompromising. M. Liaigre's interiors are so tight and precise they are the interior equivalent of La Perla bustiers. If they were any more streamlined, you couldn't get in.

Now I visited a Liaigre-designed interior the other day and I can see how these spaces may shake up your aesthetic sensibility. Everything in this tiny apartment was in black or white or understated shades of grey. (Note: Parisians don't use the words beige or grey to describe *beige* or *grey*. This is a city that appreciates a little more definition. They use synonyms like straw, string, malt, aniseed, camel, champagne and oyster shell. But I'm yet to attain to that level of eloquence.)

The focal piece was a floor-to-ceiling set of bookshelves that had been painted in glossy charcoal and now housed tomes on art and style—all with black and white covers, of course, which was very

Liaigre. The floor, meanwhile, had been sanded back and painted black, to serve as a dramatic backdrop for the pieces of furniture that served as art. It was, to use a media term, luxuriously austere.

I thought of my place, where the dimension were so small you could lie on the bed and use your toes to press the buttons on the TV, and wondered if poky studios would ever come into vogue.

Later that day I went back to my apartment, with its *merde*-brown door and the bath with the stains of its previous users still entrenched in the enamel, and sat on my white bed and looked around. My walls weren't oyster grey or church white or even the rich chocolate of a Hermès saddle; they were more of a 'rustic brown'—the brown of a wall that hasn't been dusted for fifty years. And the wallpaper, which was a velvety flock style, wasn't ornate in the current fashion for baroque elegance, but it *was* furry—though I couldn't work out whether the fur was meant to be there or had just grown all by itself over the years.

I blame the French designer Philippe Starck for this new fascination with cutting-edge design, or, as the wits term it, '*Fark*itecture' (although other wits call it 'Neo Fugly'). Before Philippe came along your taste could be a little bit daggy and no one seemed to mind. Your home could be a jumble of junk-inspired styles, and if someone did feel compelled to ask what it was all about, well, you could always pass it off as a version of 'shabby chic'. Now, if your chairs aren't Mies van der Rohe, your lounge Le Corbusier and your dining table Saarinen, there's nothing left to do but go live in Dubbo.

Let's face it—Philippe Starck has turned our lives into one gigantic, starkly minimalist frou frou–free zone. He has fairly well Starcked the world. There's barely a house left within cooee of a capital city that hasn't been redesigned with a swanky reno. God help those who want to keep their 1965 Formica and are rather fond of their 1982 leather. I'm sorry, but you'll have to go.

Colette in Paris is a perfect example of the shrines to design popping up over the globe. This store is an ode to household chic. Unfortunately, none of it is very functional, but it is still utterly irresistible, in that 'let's tease the consumer with useless stuff' kind of way. I went in there and had to refrain from purchasing completely stupid things simply because they looked gorgeous and were perfectly merchandised, even though they wouldn't fit in my apartment.

Lifestyle design is a huge trend at the moment. Huge. We are being designed to within an inch of our lives. We don't call pink *pink* anymore, we call it *fioooscha*. We don't consult our builder or architect but bring in our 'stylist' and 'gallerist'. And we no longer totter about with pot plants on weekends: we pay big-name celebrity gardeners to come in and design the space with box hedges and *beat* the garden into submission.

In order to get a grip on French interior design, so to speak, I thought I would pay a visit to my neighbour, a London architect and interior designer (apparently you do both now) who came to Paris ten years ago, took one look at French women and never left. His name is Lynton Cassell and he is well known in certain circles on the Left Bank. Mostly the female ones. Let me put it this way: Lynton's way with curves doesn't just extend to bench tops. (Well how else do you think he gets all those expensive commissions?)

He also has a *voix céleste*—a magnificent mastery of tone. Unlike some of my old editors, whose voices could open oysters, Lynton's mellifluous speech has a rich timbre that drips with money, culture, chivalry and, best of all, double entendre—one word and you just *know* he has an innate knowledge of what to do in bed.

A few days ago, I bumped into Lynton in the courtyard downstairs and so, fortified by a wine at Crémerie, plucked up the courage to arrange to visit, ostensibly to write this chapter but also to see where the city's greatest playboy lived, worked and wooed.

'How about Tuesday?' he said, checking an impressively thick black diary. 'But it will have to be in the morning. I have Madame

Fortuny and Madame Gray in the afternoon, and *les madames* don't like to be kept waiting.'

Now let me tell you a few things about Lynton before we go on. Like many men approaching forty-five with rapid force, Lynton is going through a kind of manopause. This is what happens when you're a few years short of fifty and haven't experienced everything *GQ* magazine says you should have. It's a little like that other malady, irritable male syndrome: a state of frustration that hits when you look down at your Patek Philippe watch one day and realise that twelve Armani pinstripe suits, twenty Valentino Uomo shirts, fifteen Baubridge & Kay ties and ten Hermès pocket squares do not equal personal happiness. Psychologists call it the Paris Disease, suggesting that the affliction usually hits when you realise you've spent your entire life being so busy, you've forgotten how to enjoy it.

With manopause comes a new narcissism. Men passing forty-five often run out and buy tennis club membership, or (if they have a spare million) a yacht, an island or a plane. If they're poor, they just buy a bike. They also embark on a gruelling fitness regime so they can develop the pecs they've never had in order to impress the twenty-five-year-old secretary they're about to fall into bed with.

My charming neighbour is one of these men. In the last few months he has taken to the streets, jogging. Unfortunately, he has also taken to wearing lycra under his nylon shorts, which isn't a good look for a man facing fifty. He huffs and puffs his way around the Luxembourg Gardens every morning, straining so hard it kills me to watch him.

Between you and me, it's not difficult to see that the man's swerving into a mid-life crisis.

Despite this, when Tuesday morning comes around I take a few extra minutes to dress sexily. I'm sorry. I can't help myself. I pull out a new long black skirt that I bought just for its wicked split (which says 'pretty and feminine, but you can still sleep with me if you please'), a white handkerchief linen bias-cut slip with spaghetti straps (which tend to fall down at *the* most inopportune moments) and the highest black stilettos I could find on St-Germain. It is very Monica Bellucci, very Portofino in June. Okay, so it isn't quite Paris in autumn, but I don't care. I hope Lynton approves.

At eleven I knock on the door of his apartment. Lynton answers wearing finely tailored black trousers and a white shirt with the buttons undone and the sleeves rolled back twice. If I'd owned my apartment I would have commissioned a design job on the spot. Whatever Lynton wanted, I would have pulled out a chequebook and scrawled in the noughts.

With a delicate kiss and an impressively smooth gesture of the hand he invites me in and offers me a drink.

'Whatever you're having,' I say politely, wishing I could add that the offer doesn't just extend to drinks.

While he prepares a mini *millefeuille* of vegetables—tomatoes and zucchini with mozzarella—for a light lunch, I take the opportunity to wander around and peek behind the façade.

The apartment is, surprisingly, less of a penthouse than a stylishly designed *garçonnière*, otherwise known as a bachelor pad. It is, however, far more than a studio and a place to throw down the Armani tuxedo. Like many of these handsome hideaways that are popping up all over Paris like Krug corks at a private soirée, it is a reflection of shameless egocentrism. (Although in design terms, this is marketed as 'urban masculinity'.) On one wall there is a sleek stainless steel and chocolate galley kitchen that doubles as a bar; on the other is a high-definition digital plasma screen that's the size of an exit sign on the Périphérique motorway. In between is a sophisticated chill-out space perfectly fit for undisturbed social activities. The furniture is a fusion of cutting-edge modern and elegant design classics that display a mid-century modernist's touch, while the palette is a warm shade of cognac gold. The French have a slang phrase to describe such clean, streamlined sophistication:

c'est nickel, or *c'est nickel-chrome*, which means that it has a white metal elegance that's red-hot.

It is so very stylish, and so very, very cool. I can't help but think of A.J. Baime, the articles editor for *Playboy* magazine, who once said: 'In every man, there's a little James Bond.'

Lynton mixes our drinks at the hidden bar—a startling mahogany-lined space filled with crystal glasses and top-shelf spirits—while talking in a quiet voice to someone (no doubt a female someone) on the phone. While he's preoccupied with wine and wooing, I discreetly slip upstairs. If you want to find out about a man, I say, always peek underneath the covers.

Now with some of these *garçonnière* apartments, gentlemen are finding that they're requiring a little more, er, space to entertain. As a result, many of the newer pads are being ripped apart to create more 'play room'. Some architects are even removing the second bedroom to enlarge the boudoir area.

Lynton, who obviously owned his studio apartment, had pulled his interior apart and then looked upstairs and ripped out the floor of the apartment above (which he'd obviously bought as well). The result, several impressive renos on, is an enormous 'void' (architect speak for space) and a mezzanine level that literally 'hangs' from steel supports.

I am impressed. But all I can think is that he has neutered this once charismatic Parisian space with an interior that is expensive but completely vanilla in feel.

'What do you think?' he says suddenly, coming up the stairs with two G&Ts and tapping his Gucci shoe on the cantilevered deck '*Amazing*, isn't it?'

'Yes,' I say, rendered slightly vertiginous by all the nothingness. 'It's very, er ... open?' is all I can add of the soft-loft-style interior.

'Are you mad?' he says, waving at the spatial dynamics hovering awkwardly around us. 'It's the ant's fucking Prada pants! Look at this Mies van der Rohe daybed and Corbusier couch.'

We spend the next hour debating the merits of modernist design, while I become slowly drunk on top-shelf booze.

Later that day, having learned nothing but that it is wise to date a man who knows his drinks labels as well as his clothing labels—and that most Parisians start out small with the purchase of an *atelier* and then parlay that up to a normal apartment by buying the property next door, and the one beside that, until, four apartments later they have a penthouse, if not an entire *quartier*—I weave back to my apartment, hoping the neighbours don't see me leave.

And it is then that something else I have learned occurs to me: an interior can alter your mood just as significantly as a flattering dress or a well-cut suit. In fact, its impact on your frame of mind is perhaps far stronger because, unlike an outfit, your surroundings stare you in the face every day. It is perhaps for this reason the French fill their homes with the finest, most beautiful things they can afford, even if it's only flea-market bits that make their heart skip a beat.

On Wednesday, I decide to investigate this element of French life a little more. I used to specialise in writing about architecture and interior design and was, for a time, a contributor to *Vogue Living* magazine, so you'd think I'd already be well aware of what constitutes a Parisian *salon*. But the more I amble around the galleries and side streets of the Left Bank, pausing like a poor Holly Golightly at the windows of chic boutiques, the more disoriented I feel amid all the Louis XV *fauteuils*. I'm constantly surprised and confused at how the French approach *l'art de vivre*: the fine art of living. They don't seem to create homes the way we Anglo-Saxons do, with lashings of cushions and a well-stocked drinks tray on the side. The French create spaces that are worthy of a Matisse painting.

'*Oui, bien entendu,*' says Alexandra, when I meet her for coffee at Café Palettes. 'French interior design is based on centuries of entertaining. We design to show off. Apartments are not made to be cosy. They are made to be a *gallery*. A showplace of our taste. After we finish here, I will show you. You'll see.' She puts down her cup. 'The French interior is a very complicated business. We have a saying: *à lécher les vitrines*—to lick the bibelot cabinets. I promise you, you will love what I show you so much you will be licking a lot more than that before the afternoon is out.'

Oh good, I think. I hope Lynton is one of them.

A few minutes later we're strolling along rue Jacob, Paris's answer to what to wear in the home. I feel compelled to watch, observe and learn, take notes even. And perhaps achieve some measure of credibility by applying the knowledge to my own pathetically stark studio.

'I used to write for *Vogue Living*, you know,' I say suddenly, as if it will give me some brownie points in my new design class.

'Oh?' says Alexandra, as if she can't quite believe it's true.

Part of me feels compelled to understand this aspect of Parisian living, to comprehend the complicated elements of *mode à la française*, and part of me is alarmed at how seriously they all take it. Foreigners may think that Parisians are all about *joie de vivre* but they are actually more about *savoir-vivre*. These people are so gravely determined to create stylish lives that *joie* rarely comes into it.

'The Anglo-Saxon's artistic perception of the home and the Frenchman's are completely different things,' continues Alex, as we pause before a window of well-merchandised furniture. '*Les anglais* think an interior is chic if it is cosy. Or full of dogs and cushions.' She shakes her head. 'The French value their interiors as places to create and display. *La maison* is for showing off your good taste, *n'est-ce pas?*'

'*Oui*,' I say meekly.

After I've said goodbye to Alexandra, I retire to my less-than-salubrious abode to ponder the lessons I've learned on our stroll through high style. On the internet, I find that others are considering the same subject with equal gravitas.

'Last Monday night, both the men's and women's bathrooms at

the Double Seven, an ink-and-gold nightclub on West 14th Street, carried new accessories: rolls of black toilet paper, though you could hardly see them through the gloom …' wrote Penelope Green in the *New York Times*' online edition. 'The Double Seven's bathrooms are tiled in black, have black toilets and sinks and are lighted by candles. If black is the new black, again, should its influence extend to [this]?'

It is a very good question. Could the new season's must-have really be a little black toilet paper roll?

Paulo Miguel Pereira da Silva certainly thinks so. Mr Miguel Pereira da Silva (actually, I don't know where his first name stops and his last name begins) is the president of a Portuguese paper company that makes this black toilet paper. Why, I don't know. Perhaps Paulo Miguel Pereira da Silva eats a lot of rich food? But his argument for its potential was that 'black signals avant-garde'. In a design sense, he said, it means 'irreverence'. Mr da Silva also claimed that his new product was 'neither solely a product, an object or a communication tool', but a clever combination of all three. I'll leave it to you to interpret what he meant by this.

Despite the verbal effluence, or perhaps because of it, the black toilet roll is now doing remarkably well. Orders are already coming in from New York's Double Seven, Frederick's Bar & Lounge and the basement bar at La Esquina, as well as Catherine Memmi and Stella McCartney. Black is not only the new black: it is the new loo hue.

The only trouble is, the toilet space itself—the cistern, the sink, the walls, the floor—are also turning black in this new design paradigm, so finding the paper is becoming something of an unexpected problem. Nobody can see it in the *ambiance*.

The funny thing is many French designers would not only be interested in this new loo accoutrement but would wholeheartedly support the significance of it. The toilet, after all, is just another room in the house, and every room in the French house deserves to be beautiful. Indeed, increasing numbers of French designers are now choosing to begin to design things that matter today, and for the future, rather than relying on reinventing things from the past.

As a result, Paris is changing—almost imperceptibly at first but now in leaps and well-designed bounds. A new wave of high-design boutiques, restaurants, hotels, galleries and museums specialising in *le design* are satisfying the aesthetic needs of a new generation of stylephiles and followers, and the injection of hip is giving the city a new energy and spirit.

Among these are Bon, which offers Monsieur Starck's interpretation of satin and silver, and the aforementioned Colette, which has been described as 'beyond cool'. There's also the Hôtel Costes, which has been described as 'a seraglio of swagged velvet', and a Helmut Lang boutique where the stair rail features a zipper. Now that Parisians are remembering they were once famed for groundbreaking creativity, there's no stopping their enthusiasm. Even Alain Ducasse, a man known more for his culinary talents than his interior ones, asked Patrick Jouin to add a splashy modern accent to the gilded and now slightly gauche Regency decor of his restaurant at the Plaza Athénée hotel. Design sells. Even Ducasse knows that.

Recently, French tycoon Bernard Arnault, chairman of luxury goods retailer LVMH Moët Hennessy Louis Vuitton, decided to up the ante by asking architect Frank Gehry, best known for the titanium-clad Guggenheim Museum in Bilbao, to create a new museum for the city, to be called, rather grandly, the Louis Vuitton Foundation for Creation. The ambitious request was one of the biggest topics on everyone's lips in 2006, and not just because of Gehry's mind-bending ideas for the design. A mass of wildly arranged glass panels, the new museum will apparently look a little like a crab trying to get away. Or a shattered conservatory that's been awkwardly put back together. By a blind man. Using UHU glue. Others have opined that it will resemble an insect cocoon: the strange kind you find deep in the Amazon jungle—and you're not sure if the animal is resting,

or dead. Gehry himself described his creation as a cloud—'magical; ephemeral; all transparent'—and added that he hopes young people will look at it and wonder what it is. I have no doubt they will. But there are other problems with this *musée*. Unforeseen ones. Like cleaning. According to London's Guardian newspaper, quite a number of concerned citizens were worried about who was going to look after it, and how. I mean, how do you clean a cloud? Or, for that matter, a cocoon?

But Mr Gehry refused to elaborate on the boring day-to-day logistics of his brilliant creation. Why would he? When you design a car for Porsche or Rolls-Royce, do you worry about what polish to use? *Non.* You get someone else to wipe the darn thing.

Design. Some people just don't understand.

Inspired to go and see what other wonderful and completely useless things are out there for our ready consumption, I decide to swing by Colette, one of the city's most loved stores, and a place cherished by the global *hipoisie* for its cutting-edge products and truly edgy things. But first I have to get changed, because Colette is not a place you go wearing yoga pants and a T-shirt. The place is so cool I fear I'm going to need a Hollywood stylist to help me choose the right outfit just to walk in the front door.

Like many swanky stores, Colette has one of those stream-of-consciousness taglines—*style design art food* (punctuation is obviously unimportant here)—which assures you that, when you step inside, you're being exposed to everything that matters. It is, as the fashionistas put it, 'an instant fix'. Foreign visitors often fly in and come straight here before checking into their hotel in order to feel the pulse of Paris style—just to see if it's still throbbing away. The store is a shrine to consumerism. If you want to purchase the new white-hot Nokia phone or a hot-off-the-press avant-garde Romanian fashion magazine, Colette is the place. It knows its stock is irreverent but it doesn't care. You want meaning? Go to the Louvre.

I can't help but think that Colette, the writer after whom the place is named, would be turning over in her nylon nightie. I don't think she cared much for sneakers and sportswear and I can't imagine she was overly excited by brand-name beauty products either. I suggest this to Alexandra on the mobile, when I ring her from the store to ask why I'm here. She corrects me mid-sentence.

'Colette is the founder of the place, silly,' she laughs. 'Not the famous writer.'

'Oh,' I whisper, feeling suddenly old and out-of-touch. *Un has-been.*

I decide to look cool by buying a mineral water—there are almost a hundred different types to choose from in the groovy water bar—but the selection is too intimidating. Do I opt for Cloud Juice, a composition of 7800 drops of rainwater collected in Tasmania, in a show of patriotism? Or do I top up my levels of sodium and oxygen? There are also sparkling, still or fruit water varieties to choose from. To make matters worse the merchandising is such that you can spend all afternoon just staring at the bottles. I need champagne to get over the shock of it all.

I need a visual and mental rest from all this high design and so head for home, stopping on the way to buy an old-fashioned Diet Coke in an old-fashioned bottle and sit and reflect on the way the world is changing. On the way I pass Catherine Memmi, the design store that's become the Mecca for citizens of the sixth and seventh. I can't help myself. I have to go in.

Mme Memmi, for those who are only vaguely aware of her, sits among that elite gathering of celebrity designers whose name is as familiar to the French as Madame Pompadour and Monsieur Guillotine. This pinnacle of talent includes such superstars as Andrée Putman, Christian Liaigre, Jacques Garcia and, of course, M. Starck. The difference with Memmi is that she has 'toned down' the modern look, to the relief of the sixth's and seventh's denizens, and reinterpreted it as a—how shall I put this?—a more 'comfortable' version of cutting-edge chic. (This reminds me of when Christian Liaigre asked Calvin Klein why the fashion designer had chosen him over the British minimalist architect John Pawson to work on his apartment, when Pawson's work on Klein's fashion boutiques had been so widely celebrated. The designer replied, 'Because I'm tired of sitting on a plank.')

The US magazine *Elle Décor* called Catherine Memmi the 'doyenne of poetic monochromatic minimalism' and the description is apt. While Memmi likes to keep things simple, she also does it with a certain graphic punch. She likes order and clarity and symmetry and line but she also likes the texture of modern materials, such as linen, cashmere, wood and stone, and so together the rich fabrics and the pared-down settings act as a kind of design dichotomy, calming each other and creating a pleasing scene.

I must admit I'm quite fond of Memmi's eloquent *simplicité*. If my studio were bigger than a soup bowl, I would most likely buy her things. As it is, I can't fit a candle in the place, let alone a new *chaise longue*, and so Chez Memmi will have to remain a Mecca from which I take nothing away but a new knowledge of how to dress your bedroom. Tip: expensive is the key.

There is one thing wrong with all this renewed interest in décor and *le design* and it's this: the old stores of the Left Bank—the *antiquaires* and quaint boutiques—are no longer tolerated in a city obsessed with twenty-first-century minimalism. Many of the old *antiquaires* are giving way to new avant-garde galleries that charge like a wounded bull for their abstract art, even though there's not a lot on the canvases. Gone are the cute, quirky, I-could-buy-everything-in-this-place stores you used to see years ago and in their place are spaces devoted to lines so fine you sometimes can't tell what you're buying.

On a visit to Paris several years ago, I found myself near rue

Bonaparte and detoured via rue des Beaux-Arts to see if a favourite restaurant was still there—the Restaurant des Beaux-Arts, where my former husband and I once shared the finest meal I've ever had. It was also where Oscar Wilde, Toulouse-Lautrec and many others had once eaten, storing their napkins in special drawers that were still there long after they had gone to that big restaurant in the sky. But the Beaux-Arts had gone, and in its place was a gallery so minimalist I wasn't sure what they were selling, if anything. I remember that I simply stood there sadly, scowling at the future and lamenting the past.

I leave Catherine Memmi and walk home to my own undesigned little abode. Sometimes, I think to myself as I wander through the streets, remembering the day, the rapidly changing face of design, and finally the demise of my beloved rue des Beaux-Arts, cutting-edge design can just be a cut too much.

Culinary Art

PARIS AND FOOD

If you are lucky enough to have lived in Paris as a young man then wherever you go for the rest of your life it stays with you, for Paris is a moveable feast.

Ernest Hemingway

It's easy to fall in love in Paris. All you need to do is gaze at the city's bistro blackboards. A girlfriend once told me that Paris's menus are like 'porn for professionals' and I have to agree. Just try saying some of the dishes out loud without going weak at the knees.

Saumon fumé en crème de fromage, quiche aux lardons, pâté à tresses, clafoutis pruneaux-armagnac, tarte aux noix au sirop d'érable, feuille d'automne …

Now I don't know what some of these dishes are (although I could hazard a guess), but reading them out loud is almost like reading the dirty captions or sex stories in a men's magazine. You feel as if you're doing something you shouldn't be.

Food in Paris is one of the greatest pleasures you can indulge in. People here not only understand food, they rhapsodise about it in such a way you can't help but be caught up in their enthusiasm. Even if your own aptitude for cooking is that of a blind man who's wandered onto the set of *The Iron Chef*. Restaurant menus and blackboards in France are an ode to flavour, wit, gastronomic style and culinary nous. They're also a brilliant method of education for those who want to learn French from the bottom of a plate.

I must admit I didn't know a lot about cuisine before I set foot in the bistros of this city. Which is inexcusable, really, because I come from Melbourne, a city renowned for its love of gourmet experimentation. And I have also lived for a year in Denmark, which is no slouch when it comes to whipping up a Christmas feast (or any other kind for that matter). I mean the Danes are former Vikings—they know how to lay out a dinner spread.

Even the chefs of London, where I've also spent several years, are now turning the tables (sorry for the pun) on once-stodgy British flavour and producing Michelin-class fare. And for London, that's no small feat. In fact, Londoners are going to kill me and cut me up into offal bits for saying this, but once upon a plate London cuisine was—how can I put this diplomatically?—about as delicate as its cab drivers. If you were posh you ordered *coq au vin*. If you thought you were you ordered Black Forest gateau. And if you weren't, you just ordered the fish. Wagyu beef wasn't an option. Chips, of course, were. Everything else was usually grey, soggy, uninspired and of the defrosted variety. Now, thanks to a new generation of innovative chefs like the Roux brothers, Gordon Ramsay, Nico Ladenis, Marco Pierre White and their just-as-adventurous successors, all of whom have veered doggedly away from homogeneity and steered a firm course towards the pluralistic route, London's dishes have become decidedly more daring. Indeed, London's cuisine has now become so quixotic that many are comparing the capital with its neighbour across the Channel. In spite of this, however, a prolonged period of living there still hasn't educated me in the pleasures of the plate. For whatever reason, I have never learned much about cuisine, but now, immersing myself in a city obsessed with flavour, I feel I should really try to understand what it is all about.

Paris is truly an urban *dégustation* waiting to be savoured. Unlike the rest of the world, French chefs haven't fallen prey to the string of so-called 'fashionable' gourmet fads that threaten to make great dining a thing of the past. They haven't done pan-Asian or indulged in frightening fusions (otherwise known by some chefs as 'We've got a load of lemongrass and we're not afraid to use it'), and they steadfastly refuse, bless their hot-tempered souls, to touch any kind of American-style fast food. Who wants to do that when there's so much good *French* food to enjoy?

Because of this dedication to good old-fashioned foie gras, duck confit et al., Paris has become a Mecca for a new generation of palate-driven travellers who want destinations that taste as good as they look. (This demand for destinations with gustatory intelligence has become so strong that places like Paris, Melbourne, any of the Slow Food towns in Italy and the tiny coastal village of Kinsale in Ireland are fast becoming known as 'edible cities'.) The difference between Paris and other food-obsessed cities is that here staff are almost encyclopaedic in their knowledge of cuisine and there is an almost couture-style attention to detail, while the interiors put the 'art' back into architecture and the menus constantly redefine what fine dining is. It's no wonder the phrase '*amuse-bouche*', which literally means 'to amuse the mouth', hails from here.

Traditionally, the one part of Paris that has been most proud of its culinary nous (and rightly so) is the Right Bank, but in the last few years the chefs from the *quartiers* across the Seine have stepped up to the table, strapped on a new apron, unscrewed the cigarette from their mouths and the tarte from their Tatin (even if she was extremely lovely), and sharpened their blades for a cook-off.

The result has been a slew of fabulous new eateries that are fast proving what Hemingway and Co. knew all along: the Left Bank denizens aren't bad at ripping the head off a flapping cockerel and preparing it *au vin*. And they're not too shabby when it comes to slicing the cheek of a calf and making it a delicate *tête de veau* (followed by the brain in a *cervelle de veau*). They also don't mind fiddling around with the bits of a Bresse chicken, and can do wonders with a plump Périgord duck. And I've heard it said (though I've always been too nervous to try it myself) that the *tripoux* on this side of town is a very fine version indeed. You don't know what that is? Think of mutton tripe wrapped in a chunky veal paunch. Excuse me while I just lie down and digest the idea.

Even the fashion set on the other side of the Atlantic are putting down their *Vanity Fairs* and wandering over to have a look, and that's no small thing, because the glamour and gourmet crowds don't usually share a table. In fact, there are many svelte stylephiles who haven't eaten since 1992. But now, the fashionably thin are putting their diets to one side—just for a minute, mind you—and having a nibble. Food—once considered a four-letter word in fashionese—has virtually become the accessory *du jour* at some of the city's most happening hot spots. As the old saying goes, some like it *haute*. Only here, some like it very, very *haute*.

The reason for all this action on Paris's restaurant floors is the styling. Presentation has always played a big part in French cuisine but now it's positively Lagerfeldesque. I've heard of editors who go to some of the new restaurants just to see how who's doing the design. And not only on the plates.

One of the most talked-about new(ish) places in town here is L'Atelier de Joël Robuchon: a daring venture from a chef so famous he was once crowned 'chef of the century'. This was before he declared it was all 'too much stress; I want to live', and retired. Just like that. Then, when the French had almost gotten over it—and it took a while, because the event was mourned as a national tragedy—

M. Robuchon sailed back in again with a couple of leeks and started to make culinary magic all over again. *Mon dieu*. Is there no end to the lives these French chefs have? They're more fortunate than cats.

Now I went to L'Atelier with Emily, but I don't have fond memories of the visit. I remember looking at the food and feeling like I wasn't allowed to eat. I did admire the edgy interior with its tomato-red ceilings and liquorice-black walls. But it's not much fun when you're confronted with food and can't eat a thing.

So I've decided that it might be a lovely idea to take my French friend Jean-Louis here, since he sells fresh produce at the rue de Buci market and knows a thing or two about the complexities of flavour. (I would take Eric, but I think he's still finding bits of Ulrika that he hasn't yet explored.)

We arrange to meet on Friday night, but I'm nervous because the line for L'Atelier is sometimes so long, you'd think it extends right to the Louvre. Jean-Louis is excited about going: he's not tried this famous hangout yet, despite living only a few streets away. I try to explain to him that it's a 'sort of posh sushi bar on steroids', but he waves my complaints away.

'Joël is a genius,' he sniffs. 'It cannot be that bad.'

We meet at my place, where Jean-Louis diplomatically says nothing about the absence of a kitchen, or, for that matter, a proper apartment floor plan, then set off for the restaurant. Despite having been to L'Atelier once before I can't help but feel excited in the face of Jean-Louis's anticipation.

'Come, Janelle,' he urges, as I dawdle before the traffic tearing along boulevard St-Germain. 'Hurry, hurry!'

We reach the restaurant and find ourselves inside surprisingly quickly, helped to a large extent by Jean-Louis's embarrassing elbowing through the hungry gaggle.

Once seated, I feel exhausted. Jean-Louis, on the other hand, is as jumpy as a lobster in boiling water, and declares that he is so

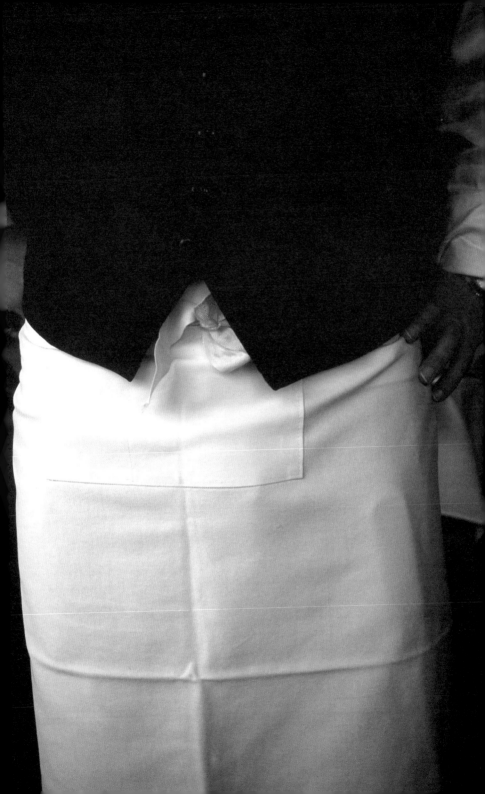

hungry he is ready to eat a horse. 'I wonder if Joël does horses?'
he winks.

We decide to start with M. Robuchon's take on a Spanish tapas
graze—the tasting menu—drawn from the chef's greatest hits. We
try a creamy chestnut soup with chunks of foie gras; a glass filled with
poached egg, wild mushrooms and cream; a toast with quail egg,
truffle, Parmesan and asparagus; and a big sea scallop with browned
truffle butter. I feel full just looking at it all. Jean-Louis, on the other
hand, is in paroxysms of admiration.

'It is genius,' he says. 'Sheer genius.'

I look around. Personally, I can't see the genius, since it just looks
like a counter with a lot of hungry people to me, but I take Jean-
Louis's word for it. Who am I to argue with a man who deals in
produce for a living?

Like fashion editors, Jean-Louis is in the business of trafficking in
taste. Basically, his job is to sniff out the next culinary trends. If he
thinks we'll be eating calf's brains next, Jean-Louis will have the sweet
potatoes to go with it. He sniffs out these trends by seeing what the city's
greatest chefs, like M. Robuchon, are coming up with. If it's a slickly
minimalist space with slickly minimalist dishes—to the point where
there's not even a smidgeon of sauce, à la L'Atelier—then Jean-Louis
will quietly take note and stock up on minimalist produce to suit.

Several courses later, I feel as though I'm about to explode. I
can't imagine eating ever again. Beside me, Jean-Louis continues to
indulge, looking up at me every now and then to nod and indicate
his approval. He hasn't said more than a few words all night. He's
been far too busy considering the ingredients and contemplating the
flavours to waste time with idle *causerie*, or chatter.

As he slurps and sniffs away, I can't seem to shake the feeling that
we're pigs at a trough, nuzzling the counter for the next feed. And it
doesn't exactly console me that I'll have to pay more than €100 for
each of us, which is at least one zero above my pay grade, when a

single punnet of strawberries from Jean-Louis's stall keeps me going for a day.

An hour later, just as my bottom is growing numb from perching awkwardly over the counter—one critic described eating at L'Atelier as 'kind of like being in heaven—only without a comfortable place to sit'—Jean-Louis decides, patting his belly with satisfaction, that he's had enough.

'Janelle,' he says, shaking his head, 'that was incredible. You are too, too generous. I will remember that for a very long time. Now. What about a drink?'

Why not? I think. We've already punished our stomachs. Why not destroy our livers while we're at it?

We head to the street and a tiny bar *ordinaire* nearby where things that come in glass are thankfully much cheaper.

'So, what did you think, eh?' says Jean-Louis. 'What did you think of Joël's magnificent dishes?'

'Well I don't normally like eating lots of food in one sitting,' I say, still trying to get comfortable in the chair, 'but I liked the presentation. The food was beautiful.'

'Beautiful?' scoffs Jean-Louis incredulously. 'That is like saying that a Gauguin is "quite sweet". Come on, Janelle. You are a *journaliste*! You can do better than that!'

I try. And I try again. But about the only thing I can think of is that the food was well styled. I know it's weak, but I feel too ill to think of anything more eloquent.

'Paris may be changing, but the food is still first class!' he declares, before issuing me with an enormous kiss on both cheeks and sauntering off into the evening, like a man at one with the world.

I watch him go, wondering if it would be too excessive to hail a taxi for only three blocks?

When I finally arrive home, having taken off my shoes to walk the last little bit, I roll into bed, staring at the brown stains on the ceiling.

I think about the fact that food is no longer just about food in the world's best restaurants. It is about art, and presentation on the plate. The old adages of *surtout, faites simple* (above all, keep it simple) and *la cuisine, c'est quand les choses ont le goût de ce qu'elles sont* (good cooking is when things taste of what they are) have been thrown out the window with the wooden spoon, and the new philosophy of the kitchen is, well, don't bother unless it looks like something you see in the Louvre. Gone are the good old-fashioned peasant dishes with simple peasant names, like *gratin dauphinois* and *ragoût*, and in their places are creations so fanciful you not only need a dictionary to translate what they are but an eye for composition to appreciate all the styling taking place on the oversized plates. A good dish now is like a mini still life, structured with colour, texture, layers and care. Woe befalls the junior chef who puts a single leek a hair's width out of place.

The trend, I realise, doesn't just stop at Joël Robuchon. It's happening right across Paris as chefs realise they have to style the food as exquisitely as they layer the flavour. At Pierre Gagnaire's respected establishment, at 6 rue Balzac in the eighth, diners are being charmed by dishes that consist of a simple giant raspberry rolled in sugar. The simplicity of it all is audacious to the point of ridiculousness, but the elegance cannot be disputed. (Gagnaire, a favourite with many in the fashion set, also does starters of hot seared foie gras balls and tiny squares of dried seaweed and grated coconut paired with bits of cauliflower. You can eat here knowing that you'll still fit into your Stella jeans afterwards.)

There is one problem with Parisian food, though, and it's a serious one. There's nowhere to go when you're tired and weary after a day of deadlines and just want a healthy takeaway to pick up on the way home. At least London's Marks & Spencer stores do pert little plastic trays of treats (I used to live on their prawn salads) that sell for under a fiver. But here, all you can do is drop by a fruit stall and purchase a banana. No wonder Jean-Louis is so happy.

I can't help but wonder if, in their single-minded devotion to food and styling and complicated layers of flavours, Paris's chefs have become exhausted. If they've done the black truffle this and the shot glass of caviar with shavings of that, and now, like the rest of us, they just want to go home to a decent feed. Like a classic roast duck. With potatoes. And a beer.

'Ah, the problem of *le takeaway*!' nods Jean-Louis when I question him about it at his stall the next day. 'French people are not used to doing takeaway like you English and Americans. We French have a word, *raffiné*, which means—' he struggles for a translation— 'refined; done with care. French people like to prepare their dishes with tenderness. They don't like to—' and here he pretends to toss a lot of things in a little plastic container, throwing his arms about dramatically—'throw food into a small box. *Non*. Food is not meant to be pressed inside plastic and then—' he pretends to shove things rapidly in his mouth—'eaten like this in front of a television! Good food is to be enjoyed; to be appreciated; to be loved. French chefs see cooking as a form of art. They are horrified by the concept of *le takeaway*.' He clicks his tongue. 'You need to come with me to the Raspail markets. I will show you how much French people love their food.'

And so, leaving his stall in the care of his uncle, who is happy to sit there and flirt with the pretty tourists, we take stroll to the famous Raspail Bio (organic) markets, for an education in the art of *le marché*.

Now I have heard much about this sophisticated place, and have even taken to strolling here when it is on. It is (supposedly) where many French and Hollywood A-listers meander for perfect produce among the beautifully arranged stalls. I always love visiting this opulent banquet and long for the day when I can perhaps say *bonjour* to Marc Jacobs while he's squeezing the melons.

The market is located on boulevard Raspail at rue du Cherche-Midi in the chic, upscale sixth arrondissement. It is the picture of what chic, upscale Left Bank *intellos* and Hollywood celebrities imagine a *marché* looks like: stylish stalls piled with irresistible produce plucked from orchards or found on forest floors and manned by charming characters straight out of a Peter Mayle novel.

Once, the very stylish, very glamorous Melbourne editor of a highly regarded style magazine, part of a worldwide group with its headquarters in New York, asked me if I knew of anyone young and diligent and chic who might want to work for the prestigious publication. They would have to be stylish and clever, she said, but they would also have to understand the importance of aesthetics. They would have to be the kind of person she could confidently send off to the Prahran market and entrust to pluck out six perfect potatoes for a photo shoot on fresh produce, for example. I've never forgotten that comment. I think it made me giggle for a week. As much as I desperately wanted to be a Voguette, the kind of girl for whom style matters more than anything, I knew I was never going to be that obsessive about aesthetics, despite half a lifetime working in lifestyle magazines. Life, I think, is far more than just six perfect potatoes.

Now, looking at this perfect market, I'm not so sure. It is so sublime that I can't help but think there is something to be said for caring about stylish fare after all. If the editor of this magazine still wanted that perfect potato, well they would most likely find it here, among the just-as-perfect stalls of this perfect Parisian place.

Under the crisp blue sky of a late autumn day we peruse the produce, which is stuffed with the fullness of the season. Jean-Louis considers each and every ripe, plump, luscious vegetable with professional gravitas, sniffing, tasting, feeling, prodding and poking. The stallholders can see they're dealing with a connoisseur—a true *gastronome*—and happily offer up their wares. We pass tables groaning with baskets full of squash, turnips, potatoes and carrots with the dirt still on them, along with wonderful home-baked pumpkin muffins and brownies in individual mini-loaf pans, stalls groaning with cheese, ducks and turkeys, and the kinds of farm-fresh milk and eggs that are only sold in the country. There are rickety crates of corn, jars of mustard sauce, wicker baskets of wild mushrooms and paper bags of purple plums. It is a bucolic scene that reflects the robust passion for food and *art de vivre* that the French have in abundance.

I read recently that old-fashioned markets such as this have had a resurgence in recent years because Parisians not only relish everything from the country—and that includes small rural producers—but they've also become afraid of the dangers of processed foods after the horrors of mad cow disease and bird flu. The demand for organic foods and *terroir* products (from 'the source') has grown so much there are now three markets dedicated to organic or bio products in Paris: Raspail, Batignolles and Brancusi.

'Markets like this are beautiful, are they not?' says Jean-Louis, smelling the autumn air. 'They are a ritual you know? We French live by the seasons. We love to buy seasonal produce. And for centuries we 'ave shopped for our produce at markets such as this.' He sniffs the air again. 'Ah, 'ow could you become tired of it? The atmosphere, the aromas, the characters? It is theatre! It is food for the soul as well as for the stomach!'

He continues his investigation of the produce and its provenance, engaging everyone he comes across in a long discussion about the origins; how they prefer to prepare and cook the vegetables; when the best time to buy and eat them is. Together, Jean-Louis and the out-of-towners discuss recipes with the kind of passion that only comes from a shared love of food, people and life. It is a wonderful sight to see.

Someone offers me a taste of organic wine and I take it gratefully. It is a big, black, full-bodied wine and full of the aromas and flavours of the countryside. I remember that an Australian wine writer, Max Allen, once described a wine as being 'chock-a-block with the flavours of late autumn—wood smoke, wet soil and ripe, sun-drenched hedgerow brambles', and sipping this, I can't help but think that this drop is as articulate.

'*Très raffiné, très romantique!*' says the *commerçant*, smiling at the look of bliss on my face. And even Jean-Louis looks pleased that I am finally beginning to understand what good food and wine is all about.

'Ah, there is a devil in every berry of the grape!' winks Jean-Louis.

It is a wine, and a day, to remember for always.

Anthony Bourdain, one of the world's greatest food writers, talks at length about the subject of produce and the magic of food in his wonderful book *A Cook's Tour*. He makes the point that memorable fare isn't necessarily the most expensive. It isn't that once-in-a-lifetime meal you have at the French Laundry or Le Grand Véfour, although dinner at places like these can indeed be memorable, if only for the bill. It's fare that grabs your imagination for a fleeting second, whether for its seasonal freshness, its flavour, or simply because it's part of the whole, enchanting atmosphere of the place where you eat or drink it. It's fare that, more often than not, sneaks up on you when you're not expecting anything special and wraps its flavour around your astonished tongue. The experience can be fleeting, and sometimes you don't even realise you're tasting something memorable and incredible until it's gone and the day is over. It's only in retrospect that you remember how divine it all was: the flavour; the freshness; the aromas drifting off down the street; the company; the calm, perfect, blue skies; the feeling of being happy.

Bourdain's perfect meal is one that finishes the book, and the cheeky chef's culinary journey across the world. It's in the West Indies, where Bourdain is relaxing with his wife after a gruelling few months of work and travel. He describes it in lavish detail: the warm, gin-clear turquoise sea; the sand between their toes; the rudimentary bar where they like to go each day to order their barbecued ribs and beer; the idea that these ribs could possibly be the best dinner in the world simply because of where they're at, both geographically and at that point in both of their lives. The food, he intimates, is good because *life* is good. Life is so goddamn sweet he doesn't know how it could get any better.

I want to raise a glass of my big, black, full-bodied wine to Mr Bourdain. I want to tell him I know exactly how he feels.

. 10 .

Paris Undressed

*A Parisian woman's money is spent on two things:
shoes and lingerie.*

Anonymous

Today I have a very important appointment. It's with a well-respected consultant who's harder to see than the Pope. This consultant runs a very successful business from behind the door of a discreet shopfront in the sixth arrondissement—a business that's frequented by half the women in Paris. So I have to keep my appointment, even if I fall off a kerb and break a leg. In fact, even if I were to be rolled into hospital following an unfortunate accident I'd just ask for an anaesthetic and hobble back down the street to see her. Because I'm dying to hear what she has to say.

This consultant knows half, if not most, of the secrets of this city—at least, the ones that slip quietly out from the most luxurious bedrooms. She not only knows who's having an affair—and who's about to—she also knows who it may be with, and what they prefer to do, er, under the sheets. Or at least what they're wearing when they do it.

You see, this woman, Sabbia Rosa, is the owner of a famous lingerie store on the Left Bank. And she knows more about Parisian women than their gynaecologists do.

Indeed, what Madame Rosa knows could wipe out half the marriages in Paris, not to mention give the media a seizure from excitement. But do you think she breathes a word? *Non*. Of course not. Because her job is to dress women for pleasure. Not to discuss whom they're having it with.

Lingerie specialists are Paris's secret therapists. They know more than all the psychologists, doctors, plastic surgeons and hairdressers put together. Many of them read the daily papers and the glossy magazines to keep, er, abreast of what's going on in Parisian society, and many of them, of course, recognise their clients in the social pages. But, being the soul of discretion, they don't murmur a thing when that client comes in the next day and quietly requests three new sets of matching knickers and bras because the others she bought last week were so surprisingly successful. Nor do they let on that they know their client is buying the matching sets for her lover and not her husband. And they would certainly never reveal that they know this because the husband has only just visited the store the week before with a *completely different woman*, to buy a *completely different* set of matching knickers and bras. Like any professional privy to confidential information, Paris's lingerie specialists keep the most intimate secrets of the city firmly under their beautifully laced, satin-covered chests.

Lingerie is one of the most important things you can invest in when you live in Paris. Lingerie and shoes. Just as nobody would dare appear in shoddy footwear, nobody would ever stoop to pulling on a pair of holey, grey, shapeless knickers. Because then you become known as someone who wears holey, grey, shapeless knickers. And that is not the kind of reputation you want to have in Paris. Those who do choose to wear holy, grey, shapeless knickers, so the reasoning goes, are just *pushing* their men into the arms of another woman. In fact, if you want to get rid of your *amour*, put your cute white knickers in the wash with a lot of dark clothes and hit the hot water button and just see what happens to your love life. Bad underwear goes against the whole grain of being a Parisian woman. In fact, most girls here would shudder at the thought of wearing cheap cotton knickers under their Marc Jacobs skirt. Seductresses do not wear baggy pants. No one was ever given a diamond or a pearl necklace from a rich Parisian lover wearing ten-year-old Marks & Spencer cottons. Women here love to flirt without shame. And it's very difficult to flirt when your knickers are creeping up your bottom or falling down around your knees.

Parisians are so fond of fine lingerie that they tend to frequent places like Princesse Tam Tam or Sabbia Rosa as often as they do the *pharmacie* or *supermarché*. (As a result, there are almost as many lingerie shops in Paris as there are bakeries.) It's almost as if they say: 'Oh, it's Tuesday? Must be time for some new lingerie …' Most of them plan ahead for the weekend, knowing that they'll probably need a set or three for the *rendez-vous* ahead. The *really* efficient ones buy enough sets to cover all their lovers, ensuring they have a little red number for the builder doing their renovations, a virginal white lace body for the businessman who flies in from England, a maddeningly sexy black set for the Italian who drops by with fresh olives and fine wine, and a cute pale pink pair for the American importer who likes his women soft, submissive and completely silent … The favourite lover gets the lingerie known as *flou*, which is all flowing and silky. The husband, of course, just gets whatever's left over in the drawer at the end of the day.

The issue of fine lingerie and what to wear when you're wearing nothing is taken so seriously in Paris that it has become a matter of national pride. Grand department stores reconfigure their floor plans just so they have ample space dedicated to the lacy intricacies of these suggestive pieces. If this wasn't thoughtful enough, there are

also dressing rooms with two different lighting schemes—day and night—so you can see how you look in any setting.

What's more surprising than the tiny tea bag–sized bras and knickers on offer for apartment-sized sums are the people buying them. There are young women with older men, 'women of a certain age' with much, much younger men, new couples who can barely keep their hands off each other, and well-dressed corporate types who tend to go for navy blue and black ensembles, to give them a lift under their corporate suits.

I was never really a serious lingerie collector when I lived in London or Australia. I was happy to have a drawer of mid-priced Simone Pérèles but I never really bothered getting into La Perla or the more luxurious labels. Paying $180 for a bra seemed a trifle excessive in my opinion—even if it did promise to reward you with a night of great sex. Now, however, I am virtually running to the nearest lingerie store and throwing down my credit card. Why? Well, the only reason a girl buys lingerie in a hurry. Because I have met a man.

I met this person last week, while I was idling near the entrance to the *métro*, debating whether to take the train to the Marais to see the Musée Carnavalet, Paris's astonishingly beautiful museum about the history of the city, thus saving the heels of my new shoes, or walk and give my calves a Parisian workout. As I loitered there for the briefest second a man came up behind me and said in perfect English: 'Madame, are you lost?' I turned to face a tall, dark-haired man in his late forties wearing a beautifully cut navy blue suit and white shirt studying me with an earnest expression. I couldn't help but think that the term 'Metrosexual' had taken on a whole new meaning.

'*Non—merci, monsieur,*' I replied in bad French, smiling rather nervously as my stomach did a turn. Looking back, I don't know what on earth I thought I was doing. Perhaps I thought I was pretending to be French? It certainly succeeded in scaring him off, anyway. He merely shrugged, smiled, and kept walking down into the depths of the station. I stood there kicking myself and hopping from foot to foot, and not just because I had aching heels from a pair of painful new shoes. (French style: I'm still getting accustomed to it.)

The thing is, I *was* lost. I was just too embarrassed to admit it. I didn't want to ask anyone. I wanted to be confident. I wanted to be *French*.

As I dawdled there, near tears, another man came up, less suave this time but still blessed with a Parisian confidence. He wasn't dapper or dashing or dripping with elegance. Nonetheless, he had kind eyes. And the kind of lovely face that you feel you could easily become friends with.

'*M'excuser, madame,*' he said kindly. '*Êtes-vous bien?* Are you okay?'

'*Non,*' I said sadly. '*Est-ce que vous pouvez m'aider, s'il vous plaît? Je me suis perdu.* Could you please help me? I think I am lost.'

He looked at me kindly, even though I'm sure he could tell I wasn't wearing silky French underwear but black cotton Marks & Spencers, and generously showed me the easiest way to get to the Marais, which wasn't very difficult at all.

And then, with the kindest of gestures, he offered to accompany me. It was one of those unexpected Paris moments where you wonder what you did to wake up and deserve it.

We went to the Carnavalet, where I was utterly enthralled by the courtyard garden and its miniature parterres and the interior with its grand salons. And then we went to dinner at a little *troquet* he knew around the corner, which was, he explained, a French abbreviation of *mastroquet*, an old-fashioned term for café, but which really meant a cosy place around the corner with good food and friendly service that only the locals know about.

After the meal we wandered outside and down to the Seine, where he talked about what he did (something in the food and wine business) and how beautiful Paris was now that Parisians had learned to enjoy it again. And then he turned and kissed me on the banks of the river, under a beautiful, crisp, winter sky as the full moon shone down making silver waves on the water.

It was lust at first moonlight.

We have met twice since then, just for coffee at the Café de Flore, and both times he has dropped everything—bags, laptop case, groceries—and cupped my face in both hands to give me a kiss. It is passion like I have never known.

And so I feel I ought to do The French Thing and stock up on my lingerie. Just in case.

Wary of doing the wrong thing in this daunting French dating game, I have decided to consult Eric—the most practised of Parisian *séducteurs*—to help me avoid any fatal faux pas.

I ask him for help, explaining the situation as best I can. He narrows his eyes. And then looks suddenly keen.

'We need to start with le Bon Marché!' he says, looking suddenly businesslike. 'And then we will go to a beautiful store I know—one that every French woman on the Left Bank goes to.'

'How do you know about it?' I say.

'Ah, I am a Frenchman. I know these things,' he says with a wink. 'Meet me tomorrow morning. I will introduce you to Sabbia Rosa.'

So here I am, dressed in my favourite black cotton undies under my favourite old jeans, waiting anxiously for a lesson in French silk fantasies.

In the hushed, luxurious interior of le Bon Marché, our first lingerie stop for the day, I feel self-conscious facing the rails and rails of ribbons and bows. Eric doesn't notice; he's too busy sifting through the racks. Eventually he pulls out a couple of navy sets and thrusts them at me.

'Navy is good,' he says confidently. 'It's sexy but still *coquette*. Try these. They should get you started.'

More than €100 later, we leave the store. As I recheck the receipt all I can think is: this better be damn good sex.

'Frenchwomen are very demanding in bed,' says Eric, 'but they can be because they know a) how to wear good lingerie so that a Frenchman falls at their feet in prayer, and b) what to do with this lingerie: how to take it off; how to *seduce*. Frenchwomen are very good at prolonging the event.' He shakes his head as if remembering every pair of French knickers that have been thrown his way. 'It is unthinkable for a Frenchwoman to rush these things.'

At €100 for a set, one would hope the sex would go on for a week.

Half an hour later we are heading to what Eric and many others consider to be The Ultimate Parisian Store: Sabbia Rosa. Sabbia Rosa is Paris's answer to an Agony Aunt. She knows everything; at least, everything to do with women and lingerie. What she doesn't know would fit on a g-string.

'Beautiful undergarments are necessary for women to feel beautiful,' she once told a journalist friend of mine. 'No matter how old you are, if you wear nice undergarments you will always feel as though you are twenty-one again!' My friend told me she felt compelled to go out and spend €300 on lingerie straight away.

The Tunisian-born Sabbia Rosa started her business thirteen years ago when she realised there was a market in Paris for beautiful lingerie. A little like the candle man who took one look at the masses in Rome and went and found a factory that made wax. Interestingly, Madame Rosa is perfectly suited to her profession. Her naturally sexy, slightly dishevelled curls and flushed skin make her look like she's just been in bed herself.

Her shop on rue des Saints-Pères is a silky haven of padded hangers with dozens of truly lascivious bras and bustiers edged in lace. It is like a naughty candy store for grown-ups, designed especially for those with a sweet tooth for colour. And other pleasures of the eye. She obviously knows her stuff. Those who have been to see her include Dustin Hoffman and Cindy Crawford. Although not together, presumably.

I pause before a scalloped demi-cup bra. It is heaven on a coat hanger. A little further along there are pale pink and mint-green sets that remind me of the macaroons at Ladurée. I never wear green and rarely wear pink but somehow these look delectable and delicious and utterly divine. I am instantly addicted. Sabbia Rosa is about to become the underwear version of my dealer.

I once read that the difference between French lingerie and Italian is 'subtlety'. Italian lingerie is more elaborate, and slightly wicked in its use of satin and bows. It's out-and-out suggestive. French lingerie, on the other hand, is about understatement. It's decadent but still dignified. Feminine rather than *femme fatale*. The fabrics are usually first-class and the workmanship is detailed. It's less about adornment than design. Preferred colours include champagne, pale candy pink, elegant navy, sea-foam green, Tiffany blue and tangerine for weekends under jeans. Parisians don't care much for yellow, or, strangely enough, for black, unless it's trimmed with a little cream antique lace or tiny silk-covered buttons. White is normally embroidered or edged with ruffles of white eyelet. Silver or gunmetal grey, however, is surprisingly popular, perhaps because it's perfect for business as well as for play.

According to an industry report, French women apparently spend 20 per cent of their fashion budget on lingerie. Those styles flying out the store and into the bedroom, according to this same report, include moulded shapes with naive embroideries; classical demi-cups with visible underwire; transparent bodysuits; and both bandeau and triangle brassieres.

I take my new purchases (I have bought the Ladurée-green and pink set) and, thanking Eric—who hasn't provided much support all day, at least not the kind that comes in lace—saunter happily down the street with my new lingerie. I don't know if it will guarantee me romance. But it certainly makes my day.

Now all I need is a new pair of shoes to complete the picture.

I once read a list compiled by Forbes.com, one of my favourite business websites, of '100 Things That Were Worth Every Penny'. Included in this curious and strangely absorbing list were built-in bookshelves, a business adviser (not a partner, interestingly enough), Baccarat wine goblets and a La Perla bra. The list also include Petrossian caviar, any Leica camera, a Macintosh Powerbook, a housekeeper, a Van Cleef & Arpels emerald-cut diamond engagement ring, a custom-made tuxedo, any pre-1989 Porsche 911, any seventies vintage BMW motorcycle and a good divorce lawyer. Followed by a good pillow.

Now I love and covet all of these things—well, perhaps not the divorce lawyer—but it was the bra that really caught my interest. How could a slip of lace possibly be considered a luxury? I wondered at the time. Especially when it was usually never on long enough to be appreciated. Don't get me wrong—I love the elegance of a gorgeous bra as much as the next girl. But I don't think lingerie makes you walk as sexily as a great pair of shoes, for example. I don't think it makes you as confident as a pair of wickedly high heels.

Some time ago, Australia's ABC radio devoted an entire program to the seemingly innocuous subject of shoes. The producer in charge of the show pulled together an impressive panel of commentators, including a couple of bespoke shoemakers, style commentator and author Maggie Alderson (former editor of British *Elle* and now fashion columnist for Australia's *Good Weekend* magazine), and Lydia Kamitsis, then head curator of the Musée de la Mode et du Textile at the Louvre. Together these self-confessed shoe-obsessed professionals discussed everything from glass slippers to red shoes (the kind that spell trouble straight away), and—most fascinating of all—the drawers of shoes that rest in 'shoe heaven' in the basement of the Louvre. The final verdict of the show? Shoes still offer the ultimate feel-good factor. As a friend of mine says, they lift more than just your self-esteem.

Shoes are everything. Perhaps even more than lingerie. And nowhere is this understood more than in Paris, the city of the sexy stiletto. Okay, so some people are passionate about matching bra and knicker sets, while others seduce their men with top-drawer bodies (their own, as well as the lace versions offered by Sabbia Rosa). But I think if you asked Parisian women to choose between their lingerie and their shoes, their hands would linger on their shoes. French shoes are fabulous redefined.

I had heard the myth of the French heel long before I came to the country. I went to school with a girl who was a member of the famous Rothschild family, and who regularly flew back to France to visit her family's estate. Her mother was always coming home with suitcases full of shoes. 'I love Australia,' she cooed to me once, 'but your footwear is *terrible*!'

So naturally the first thing I did when I landed in the city as a sixteen-year-old student was seek out a shoe shop. I wanted to see if they really were as divine as my friend's mother said they were. I finally found a store on the Champs-Élysées. Inside were shelves and shelves of *the* most incredible shoes. Shoes you would sell your boyfriend to Paris Hilton for.

Two decades on, I would still sell my boyfriend for a single pair of French-crafted shoes. And I'm not the only one. Parisians *adore* their footwear. Indeed, shoes here are considered so seriously they're almost the key to social acceptance. If you don't believe me, step out in a Paris street in shoddy heels and note the service you receive. Then wear a drop-dead gorgeous pair the next day and see if your life doesn't change.

I remember staying at a beautiful boutique hotel near the Eiffel Tower one year and spending the first three days wearing flat ballet pumps. I was there to write several stories for a couple of magazines and so spent virtually every day, all day, rushing around the city on foot. I simply could not have survived in heels. Certainly not the kind that make your calves look like Elle Macpherson's and your swagger resemble Naomi Campbell's. I would have fallen flat on my face in the first two hours.

But on the fourth day I had a morning free and so, tired of tugging on black pants and shoving my feet into (by now slightly odorous) black ballet pumps, I tried to coerce my tender soles into a pair of ladylike kitten heels. I stumbled downstairs to the reception for breakfast and slid gratefully to the nearest chair, wondering if it wasn't wise to go back to my room and get changed again.

Suddenly the owner, who had barely said ten words to me the entire stay, rushed over to compliment me on my shoes, as if he had never expected this grubby Australian journalist to, as they say in the bush, 'scrub up with any effect'.

For the next hour he couldn't do enough for me. And all the time he kept staring at my feet. I tell you, those shoes were the key to everything that day.

The whole experience was, admittedly, slightly unsettling. I'm still surprised that he didn't throw me out when I first checked in. I can almost imagine him looking down at my scruffy heels and saying, 'Oh, I'm sorry, madame, but we don't have any rooms. At least, none for those appalling shoes.'

So what is it about French shoes that make women weak at the knees? Well, I'll tell you. French shoes are architecture for the legs. They make bad ankles look beautiful and slightly round calves look sleek. They take a dress and lift it into the glamour league, and they do it all—the *séduction* and the provocation and the tease—without ever looking too cheap. They can also give a kick to a business suit and make a simple white dress into a Marilyn Monroe-style birthday present for President Kennedy. If Elizabeth Hurley were stepping out to launch her career today, she would most likely choose French shoes rather than safety pins to make a memorable media entrance.

The most beautiful French shoes in my opinion are those made

by Christian Louboutin. Somehow he makes even a flat ballet pump look positively seductive. His towering creations all have a signature red leather sole, so when you're in a jazz club or a swanky restaurant looking around at all the elegant patrons, you can always tell who's a Louboutin lover. It's there in black and red on the bottom of their feet. (Sarah Jessica Parker memorably teetered around Paris in sky-high Christian Louboutins for the finale of *Sex and the City*.)

But Louboutin is not the only one dressing the slender heels of Parisians. There's also Rodolphe Menudier, Charles Jourdan, Michel Vivien and Pierre Hardy. But the party girls' favourite would have to be Bruno Frisoni, who offers playful shoes that say 'look at me: kiss me: take me home tonight' with nothing more than a striped ribbon bow.

Now, are you getting my drift about Parisian shoes?

Once I did a photo shoot in London with a French model who had just spent her first cheque on the most eyebrow-raising, wickedly decadent pair of French heels. In Australian dollars, I think they were around $1500. But I don't know. There could have been an extra nought on that. Anyhow, she was so in love with her sexy new shoes that she refused to take them off, even when the stylist told her that some of outfits didn't go with them. The model pouted; the stylist pleaded, the photographer grew tetchier with every second. Finally, the model came up with a solution. She would simply wear her shoes and nothing else. The photographer, looking like he had died and gone to heaven, looked eagerly at the stylist, who shrugged and slunk to the back of the studio with an expensive Valentino gown. So the photographer shot the model in nothing but her new shoes, with the clothes hung on a mannequin and a metal rail behind her. Back at the magazine, the editor who was paying for it all thought it was inspiring, and put the shot on the cover.

There is just one problem with all this architectural elegance for the feet, however, and it's a significant one. Paris simply isn't built for beautiful, high-heeled shoes. There is the city, with all its cobblestones and kerbs and pedestrian bridges, and there are the shoes, with their towering heels and intricate engineering, and the two simply don't get on.

Because of this issue, a particular style of shoe has come to prominence in the city over the last year or so—a shoe that is far less vertiginous than the typical Parisian heel and thus enables Parisian women to walk very fast, as they like to do. This shoe is the ballet flat.

'Flat pumps are much better to wear in Paris because heels are too hazardous,' says Alexandra, when I ask her about the issue over a hot chocolate at Ladurée one day. 'Some women will wear heels but only when they're getting a taxi to go and visit their lover. Otherwise, we prefer flat pumps. It's easier.'

Admittedly, on French women like Alexandra, the flat, particularly the ballet flat, doesn't look flat at all. It looks stylish, intellectual, bohemian, offbeat. It brings to mind Audrey Hepburn in *Funny Face*, Jean Seberg in *À Bout de Souffle* and Bardot in the sixties. It is very Kate Moss; very Vanessa Paradis.

'It's sort of a heel for highbrows,' agrees Emily, later in the day, when I ring to ask her opinion. 'The ballet flat is the most adored shoe in Paris at the moment. You can wear it under jeans and still look intelligent and sophisticated. It's for modern-day beatniks.'

Sadly, I have only ever been able to wear ballet flats under jeans and Capri pants, since they can make your legs look short. And not very French. But I agree with Alexandra: they are so comfortable racing around the streets of Paris that it's difficult to go back to wearing heels.

The ballet slipper may be flat but it might just usurp the famous Parisian slingbacks and stilettos yet. As Alexandra says, 'French women love high heels but they are best left to the catwalk, the restaurant and bed.'

. 11 .

Romance

AND THE FOOD OF LOVE

I'm looking for love. Real love. Ridiculous, inconvenient,
consuming, can't-live-without-each-other love. And
I don't think that love is here in this expensive suite
in this lovely hotel in Paris.

Sarah Jessica Parker in *Sex and the City*

Many years ago, I went on a date with an Englishman who took me
to see the play *Closer* by Patrick Maber. For those unfamiliar with this
now-cult production, which was eventually made into a film with Julia
Roberts, it is a bruising, unblinking dissection of modern relationships
in the age of divorce and internet dating. It is also about that hotly
debated topic, love—although it tends to use an awful lot of f-words
to navigate the issue. Everyone was talking about this play in London
at the time because the dialogue was a step down from a pornathon
in some parts. Because of this, the theatre was packed. You couldn't
have got any *Closer* if you'd tried.

As the play unfolded it became clear that it was a modern-day tale of romance for the jaded generation. When the character of Dan, a writer, asked Alice, the stripper what she wanted—what she *really* wanted—she replied simply: 'To be loved.' And when she added sadly, 'It's a big want,' you could feel the whole theatre shudder in sympathy.

My boyfriend, who wasn't really a boyfriend at that stage, just a lovely promise of one, sat beside me without moving a muscle. It was as if the play resonated with each and every person in a way they hadn't expected, but nobody knew how to react.

We sat there the whole time, he and I, not touching, not even holding hands, which I thought was strange considering the play's title. When the curtains finally closed he turned to me.

'Drink?' he said.

'Yes,' I replied politely, thinking, as everyone else probably was, that sex would be far more preferable.

As we stepped outside, the crowd seemed to dissolve in the night air. It was as if everyone who had came to the play to see some hot action and instead witnessed little but four characters talking about the f-word a lot had rushed home to re-enact their own *Closer*.

Not really knowing what to do, perhaps because we were both quite polite and therefore not the type to suggest anything other than coffee and a brioche to finish the night, we wandered up to Soho to find somewhere to eat. Halfway up the street, he took my hand. I remember that moment to this day. Three hours after the play started, we were finally getting *Closer*.

It was a lesson in how the English approach dating: with guarded emotions and unfailing politeness. Think of the Queen and you'll have some idea of how much of the country behaves.

French people, on the other hand, approach dating with the same passion they give to everything else in their lives. Think of how they converse. Gesticulating is just the start of the game.

Because of this Latin passion and open manner it is not uncommon

in Paris for a complete stranger, if he finds you *séduisante* (appealing),
to stop you on the street and say, '*Excusez-moi, mademoiselle* ... Do
you have a light/the time/a moment for a coffee/an evening free for
dinner?' A girlfriend of mine was once stopped and asked for her hand
in marriage. And she's pretty sure he wasn't joking.

Like their Italian cousins across the border, Frenchmen think
nothing of initiating contact with a girl on the street, in a store, or in
a corner of a bar, and for their part, Frenchwomen think nothing of
responding to it. In fact, they adore it. They don't leave the house
without their lipstick on for this very reason. Unlike in some Anglo-
Saxon countries, there is no dancing around the issues of dating or
romance—no second-guessing what someone means, and whether
'coffee' means 'just coffee' or something else entirely. And unlike in
some Anglo-Saxon countries there aren't a dozen 'steps' between the
first smile and the initial dinner. That would be a waste of time, say the
French. In Paris, time is short. One just plunges right in.

There is, however, one small rule in the French dating game.
It is always up to the man to initiate the *séduction* and the romance.
It does not do for a woman to say an unsolicited *bonjour*, even if she
thinks someone has given her a cheeky grin from across the street.
Frenchmen are old-fashioned, after all. They like to be the ones doing
the chasing. In this way, French dating hasn't changed a lot since the
twelfth century. *L'amour courtois* still holds strong.

Knowing all this, I am reluctant to appear too forward with my
new French boyfriend in case it is misinterpreted. I don't want to be
the first to suggest advancing from coffee to dinner, even though I'd
like to go out for a proper, candle-lit time.

And so I wait, clinging desperately to my new French patience as
the Sabbia Rosa lingerie burns a hole in my *armoire* drawer.

Besides, there are a lot of things about French romance that I am
still to learn. Kissing is just one of them.

When I first arrived in Paris, at the tender age of sixteen, I was astonished by the number of people kissing, hugging and generally showing affection for each other's bits in public. Parisians couldn't get enough of each other. Lovers would clasp in Doisneau-style embraces outside the *métro* stations, or line the Seine, legs intertwined in passionate links, so that you had to detour around them. *Grandes dames* catching up for tea at Angelina would kiss elegantly before they sat down to discuss their grandchildren. Old men meeting for card games under the trees in the Luxembourg Gardens would grasp each other with barely contained glee and smack each other on both cheeks with their blistery old lips. And on the tiny side streets near St-Germain-des-Prés, where it doesn't do to stop suddenly in a car because you're liable to cause an accident or four, people would slam the brakes on their little cars in order to roll down the window and greet friends on the street—to which the friends would exclaim '*Bonjour*' and bend down to give them a kiss on each cheek. Even guys in the bars of St-Germain would shower each other with backslaps and double-kisses to show they were in touch with their passionate French side. The city was literally charged with love.

The great French singer and actor Maurice Chevalier once explained the French behaviour of kissing with wild abandon by putting it down to an enthusiasm for renewing friendships.

'We like to renew acquaintances, we Frenchmen,' he said. 'We will kiss a man we haven't seen for five years—or a girl we haven't seen for five minutes!'

When you're a foreigner, however, and unsure about the customs of kissing people, the tradition can seem quite daunting, especially at New Year's Eve parties, when the smooches flow like *vin rouge*.

The thing is, you simply have to get used to it, because kissing is part of the daily interaction in Paris. It's fairly much par for the course among the twenty- and thirty-something generation, even when meeting friends of friends for the first time. A Parisian greeting is as warm as they come.

I have to admit, I don't mind the Parisian kiss. It allows you to connect with people. Once you've mastered the back-and-forth movement that goes on, the swivelling of heads and neat missing of lips, it can be a lovely way to meet people. It also allows you to have a French kiss without having to have a French kiss, if you know what I mean.

But kissing isn't the only way the French show their passion for each other. Food is another big part of the romance game. In fact, *l'amour et la table*—the acts of eating and making love—are, in many French eyes, intimately linked. Where there is food, say the French, there is bound to be love and lust. In fact, such is the connection between the two that certain foods, including bananas, turnips, cucumbers and zucchinis, are all metaphors for *le sexe*, or *le pénis*. I once met a girl at a party who kept talking about her new lover—a *charcutier* she'd met while shopping at a street market. 'His *andouillette* is very good,' she said with a wink. And she wasn't just talking about his sausage. If you wonder why some French shopkeepers close their stores for a few hours at midday, well, now you know why. They're not having a siesta. There is an old French saying that goes: 'You ask why we close the shop at lunch? Because the table is just the right height.'

A year or so ago, the British *Observer* ran a story about the kind of restaurants that are best to have an illicit *rendez-vous* in. Naturally, the French ones won hands down. Something to do with all that saucy action. French is the language of gastro-naughty. Just think of *coq au vin*.

The most important part of a meal, if you're dining to seduce—or, indeed, be seduced—is dessert. Dessert signals the end of the dinner and the possibility of something a little more decadent. After all, one can't just leapfrog straight from the *filet de boeuf* to the boudoir. You need a teaser, a culinary segue—preferably something with a little whipped cream, some flaky pastry and chocolate on top. Something that might, if you're a girl, and also very lucky, drip down your décolletage, so that you have to slyly wipe it off, with much licking of your fingers. Oh? Did I just drop chocolate on my cleavage? Oh my.

Seductive French desserts include *bavarois* (a moulded egg custard, served cold with whipped cream), *millefeuille*, *religieuse* (two balls of choux pastry filled with butter cream), and, naturally, a *tarte Tatin*. But the most titillating dessert is probably the *boudoir*, which is a lady's finger biscuit. Nothing more needs to be said on this matter. The visual image tends to speak for itself.

I have never been much of a gourmet. I'm not someone who's charmed by the kind of romance that's served *à la française*—with asparagus tips and *sauce hollandaise*. In fact, I can usually be wooed, to a certain extent anyway, with a *vin ordinaire*. So when my new Frenchman finally offers to take me out to dinner at another *troquet* he knows, I am in two minds. I'd like to go out for a proper, candle-lit time, wearing my new lingerie. But I worry, like a polite girl, that the expense will be wasted. It will be like taking a blind person to see the Louvre.

Nevertheless, I accept. Because I am in Paris. And because I am in the mood to be seduced.

Now there are those restaurants that are tailored, ever so subtly, for females (those with cute powder rooms; those with fancy drinks with just-as-fancy names; those with ornate furnishings and swathes of style) and there are those restaurants that are tailored a little more to men (those with timber wall panelling; those with cigar bars; those with scantily clad girls carrying silver trays). Even those restaurants that don't deliberately lean towards a certain customer may find that their menus attract one or the other anyway. This is because men and women view dining differently. Women like long menus that stretch on for pages and are full of dishes described with sophisticated whimsy and wit. We want to know the provenance of everything: has the beef been grain fed, are the chickens are free range, does the farmer makes tender love to his wife at the end of the day? Men, on the other hand,

just want to know how big the steak is. Furthermore, girls don't like seeing certain things appear on their plates: animals with their faces still attached, for example—especially the eyes. And we certainly don't like, or at least don't like to be seen, tucking into anything that was once an orifice. That includes pig's ears. We like thin, flat things, like carpaccio or sashimi, that you can't quite tell have once been walking, or fishing, or flying freely above in the bright blue skies. It's difficult to find a good restaurant that caters to both sexes. But my new man, Christian, has managed to find one. His cosy little *troquet* turns out to be Lapérouse.

Lapérouse, on the quai des Grands-Augustins in the sixth, is one of the world's most romantic restaurants. For decades this seventeenth-century Seine-side haven has been favoured by lovers new and old for its private dining rooms and decadent, dimly lit, intimate interior. These 'secret' salons helped make Lapérouse the centre of literary and political Paris in the late 1800s, when private affairs, business and otherwise, took place in the private, *boiserie*-graced spaces. Famous regulars included Emile Zola, George Sand, Alexandre Dumas and Victor Hugo. It was also famous for being the preferred place for politicians to take their mistresses for a secret *rendez-vous* amid the *belle époque* opulence. The latter would use the restaurant's mirrors to ensure the diamonds given to them by adoring lovers were indeed real. It didn't do to take jewels at face value, after all.

As well as being favoured by mistresses, Lapérouse is also appreciated by men because it does handsome, grand, manly dishes like game, beef fillet and saddle of rabbit, not to mention crayfish bisque flavoured with Szechuan pepper. This is a menu full of rich, hearty dishes to match the rich, hearty prices. You won't find carrot and apple juice with a side serving of seaweed on this menu. There may be models dining here, but they're too busy eyeing off the sapphire rings their wealthy old industrialist boyfriends are giving them to worry about the food.

With the glistening glasses of wine, the flash of dignified, limitless credit cards and the hefty serving of nostalgia, it is grand Paris dining as you dreamed it would be. No wonder romantics love it.

Christian, to my surprise, has booked one of the private salons, which includes, to my surprise, a couch as well as a table. I discreetly ignore this, even though it spells S-E-X before we've even started the oysters. It is surprisingly distracting having a couch in the background when you're trying to carry on a conversation. It's a little like dining in the bedroom, on a picnic table at the end of the bed. The suggestion is less than subtle—especially when you don't know your companion very well. I'm almost waiting for him to say: 'So? Shall we start with an entrée? Or shall we just skip to the sex?'

I take a seat, fascinated by the scratches made by countless diamond rings in the mirror, and wish that I had an Elizabeth Taylor-style gem to graffiti my name in the corner.

'Do you drink wine? Would you like a bottle of Château Margaux to start with?' says Christian, suddenly formal and businesslike, perhaps to distract us from the winking settee.

'Thank you. That would be lovely,' I reply, suddenly out of my depth.

We hear a polite cough, and realise it's the discreet warning of the waiters as they approach our private dining room. For some reason, this alarms me even more. I feel like saying: 'We've only just met! We won't be doing unmentionable things yet!'

Christian orders for both of us: we have a dish of crab, followed by Scottish grouse. Then we share the Margaux. It's a '98.

Halfway through the bottle he drops the bombshell.

'Do you know that I am married?' he says quietly.

I almost spit out my Margaux.

'I'm sorry?' I say, wondering if the alcohol was more potent than I thought and that perhaps I'm imagining things. Including the settee.

'I'm married,' he repeats. 'Most well-educated Frenchmen in their forties are.'

'Is that right?' I reply. 'And what do these well-educated, forty-something Frenchmen think they're doing taking single, thirty-something girls to very expensive restaurants for dinner?'

'It is what we do,' he says simply.

I don't know what to say. I am obviously so far out of my comfort zone I have wandered into another level of ethics altogether.

'You know, I really like you. I think you are *très enchanteresse*,' he says, perhaps to break the icy silence that now threatens to chill the wine. 'Adultery is not a bad thing, you know. It is *normal* in Paris. Everybody has affairs. I know you are shocked, my beautiful girl, but really, it is no big deal. The French have always been able to deal with *les liaisons amoureuses* better than the English. *Le cinq à sept* is the time of day when all those who can slip away to have a quiet moment with the people they love. Don't you know that's why French politicians keep *garçonnières*? It is what keeps us French people sane.'

I don't know what to say to this either. It is all too foreign for my Anglo-Saxon tastes. I had heard about Frenchmen like this—*les honnêtes hommes*, they call them, these suave, educated, intellectual and worldly gentlemen who are not quite honest but nevertheless exude an irresistible charm that draws you in. I just never thought I would come across one so soon.

I take another sip of the famous wine and suddenly feel, with a quiet shudder, that I don't want to taste any more. It is all too much: the Bordeaux; the hard-hitting dishes; the private room; the *chaise longue* in the corner; even the expensive lingerie. All I really want to do is find a nice, *single* Frenchman, go to a cute bistro, and sit and chat over a *pinard*—a *vin ordinaire*—and *une blanquette de veau* (the French version of a parma and a pot). I don't want fancy. What I want—what I've always wanted but just failed to recognise it—is a simple, uncomplicated, refreshingly trouble-free relationship. I want the kind of romance that comes with a little *troquet*, complete with red and white checked tablecloths and a blackboard full of homemade fare. I want the kind of romance that comes with white cotton knickers—the kind that look beautiful with your boyfriend's white shirt when you wake up: put it on over your naked torso, roll up the French cuffs and have breakfast with him the next day.

'You know, I could very easily marry you,' says Christian.

'Well, that's a shame,' I say, setting my oversized white napkin down. 'Because you're already wed.'

And then I stand gracefully—at least as gracefully as I can with two glasses of very fine Margaux tucked under my lacy French lingerie—and walk calmly out of the salon.

French liaisons, I decide as I hail a taxi to take me back to the *quartier* Odéon, are intricate and knotty and full of twists and turns. Not to mention couches in the corner. And I just don't feel, even with all my new Parisian *savoir-faire*, that I'm quite ready for such complications yet.

As I'm driven home by a chatty taxi driver, with the lights of Paris winking suggestively at me from behind, I feel a little lacklustre, as if I've somehow let my French friends Alexandra and Simone down. I'm sure they would be telling me to 'go for it'; to acquire that sapphire ring and anything else that comes with it. (As in a car; an apartment; a little yacht at St Tropez …) But I just can't do it. Some French women may seek out silk and satin sets and sex with *les honnêtes hommes*, but I'm a little bit more traditional, I'm afraid.

L'hiver et Mélancolie

FINDING SOLACE IN THE DEPTHS OF A PARISIAN WINTER

Paris is a hard place to leave, even when it rains incessantly and one coughs continually from the dampness.

Willa Cather

There is a time of the year in Paris when the darkness falls onto the city and settles in for good. It's usually around late November or December, although it can be earlier, depending on the autumn. You don't notice the lingering gloom and the diminishing days for the longest time because you're so wrapped up in the end-of-year activities: the Christmas gaiety in the bars and bistros, and the lights twinkling in all the stores. And then one night when you're hurrying home you remember that you haven't seen the sun in a while. It hasn't been light in the mornings when you've woken up and it's barely shown its face during the day, even when the clouds thin out and become white rather than grey. It's then you know that *l'hiver*—winter—has arrived.

It was hard to say exactly when winter came to Paris this year.

It just sort of slid into the city one frosty Sunday morning when everyone was still asleep, glazing the streets and the grass in the parks with ice and turning the Seine a mournful shade of beige. The sky became an ominous steely grey and the cold came in, brutal and relentless, on a gust of wind. The chill was so biting you could feel it whip the profanities from your throat, snap them in two and send them scattering and clattering down the street. Those who were awake, either at Christmas parties that had persisted until the early hours or at home, waiting for the first yawn of dawn, faced the thick darkness with a shudder and felt instantly unsettled. It was an undeniably menacing introduction to the months to come.

That was a week or so ago. And it still feels as though Paris is struggling to fit into its new winter coat. Everywhere you go people mumble and complain about the cold and the dark, and the streets feel strangely quiet. You can't help but feel sad, as if something good is coming to an end.

This morning, as the city slumbered, trying to forget its winter depression, I woke early, tired and tender after a fitful night. I have been waking early for the past few weeks and I'm not sure what's causing this cyclical insomnia. I hope that it isn't regret.

Isn't it funny how you can go through thirty years with a healthy attitude of *je ne regrette rien*, and then, as you grow older, and perhaps also (hopefully) a little wiser, start feeling the pangs of regret for the things you haven't done or said? Regret is a powerful stimulant. It can keep you awake at night for years if you're not careful.

Unable to return to sleep this morning I padded to the window and looked out. In the brittle white of the winter night the world was quiet and still. So I decided to find some warm boots and venture out for some fresh air. There is nothing like a deep lungful of winter air and a brisk walk through the early morning streets to cure a painful case of remorse.

So I dressed and went outside, feeling the cold seep through my coat. Above me, the morning sky was turning to an insipid grey-blue shade with the early light, and in the Luxembourg Gardens, the first of the city's joggers had started to appear on the gravel paths, like ghosts in the dawn light.

It was such a stark change from the Paris I knew during summer and autumn that it was difficult to believe it was one and the same place. Last month the city was magnificent. The streets and stores were starting to show the first signs of Christmas, the bars and bistros were filling up with workers noisily celebrating the end of the year, the jazz clubs winked at passers-by with neon signs that announced, in a sexy serif font, that some deliciously beautiful, deep-voiced singer was gracing the stage that evening, and the restaurants hung out irresistible Christmas menus that promised a great meal with every mouthful. The city felt full of cheer and promise.

But now those streets were empty, and distressing. Even though Christmas was just around the corner, Paris felt spiritless. The soul had departed the city, no doubt bound for warmer climes.

The vision of the joggers haunted me as they drifted like grey ghosts through the Luxembourg Gardens. I sat there on a bench and, as I watched them, I could begin to feel my own ghosts creep up and tap me on the shoulder—the ghosts of my childhood, and my early twenties, and even my thirties. The ghosts I had tried to repress for so long—the ghosts I had tried to ignore—hoping that if I did they would eventually disappear and never bother me again. But now, in the thick melancholy of a grey Parisian winter, they were materialising again, haunting my days and my dreams.

These ghosts are many and varied, but the most persistent of them are the ghosts of children I'll never have. The sadness of this fact overwhelms me so much I often have to stop, catch my breath and compose myself, so I don't tumble headlong into tears. It usually happens around Christmastime, when mothers and fathers take their beautifully dressed families shopping for Christmas gifts.

You see them in Paris's department stores, deliberating between a book about monsters and a brand new teddy bear. You see the fathers lift their daughters into their arms and whisper secrets in their ears. You see mothers speaking earnestly to sons, imparting some snippet of motherly advice. You see them leave, heading for a hot chocolate at Angelina, or a ride on the Ferris wheel at the Tuileries. And you know, with a bolt of sadness, that you will never have the same experience.

The absence of children is something only those who have been unable to conceive can really understand and appreciate. It is a loss that lingers for years, and it is even more tragic for those who have either miscarried or aborted children early in their lives. The discovery of infertility years after you've terminated the only child you will ever have hits you like a punch to the face. As Hilary Mantel put it in her memoir *Giving Up the Ghost*, 'if [children] are aborted or miscarried or fail to materialise at all, they become ghosts within our lives. In a sly state of half-becoming, they lurk in the shadow land of chances missed.'

A few years ago, a generation of successful women who had spent their lives chasing deadlines rather than boyfriends and creating financial security rather than candle-lit opportunities for conception with their partners were shaken by the release of a book called *Baby Hunger* by American author Sylvia Ann Hewlett. Hewlett had discovered that childlessness was becoming a shockingly common problem for a great number of busy professionals in their thirties, most of whom had assumed they would simply fall pregnant when the time was right. And when life didn't quite happen as they expected, usually because they were too busy working, or had suffered some silent illness that had made them infertile, such as pelvic inflammatory disease, they couldn't understand why. They were, said Hewlett, beside themselves with grief, guilt, pain and regret. Naturally, all those who were heading towards their late thirties and hadn't made plans for a family, usually because they were too busy making plans to become a

CEO or the owner of their own company, bought the book and read it in a panicked fashion from cover to cover. The reaction was nothing short of collective terror. The media, of course, picked up the issue and, before long, the dilemma of the childless female was splashed all over the newspapers and magazines with as much drama and column space as the war in Iraq. It was, said many commentators, feminism swinging back and stinging itself, like a scorpion's tail. We women thought we could have it all, did we? Well, well. Look what your career was doing to you. What use was feminism now, hey?

One of my girlfriends, a stupendously successful restaurateur, discovered she was infertile just at that point in her early thirties when she wanted to slow down and make time to have a baby. She became so determined to prove the sceptics wrong and show that women could indeed have it all, she spent thousands of dollars having her eggs frozen in the hope that some innovative scientist would figure out how to remedy the situation before she was too old to enjoy the experience. She's still confident there will be an answer. And indeed many geneticists predict that it will be routine for future generations to put their eggs on ice and continue working until these women decide on the best time to start a family.

I'm not one of these optimists. I don't want to put my hope in a laboratory. I don't want to go through the pain of IVF. And I'm starting to doubt that I have the mental energy to even go through adoption. Even if I was young enough to make freezing eggs an option, I've now reached the stage where I would rather put a bottle of bubbly on ice than a couple of potentially ineffectual eggs. After years of torment and regret, I'm finally coming to terms with this unexpected loss in my life. And I'm now trying to be kind to myself. Part of this means letting go, and moving on. It means remembering the joy to be had in living, even if there are no little bodies crawling into bed to share it with me.

Now, as I sit here on a cold bench in the Luxembourg Gardens, the damp seeping into my jeans, I can feel the ghosts come swirling around me again. But it's fine. For the first time in my life, it's completely fine. I am happy to let them come. Because I know how to acknowledge them and how to send them away. With a little smile and a wave. I know that they will continue to come but that, with time, they will come less and less, and eventually they'll fade away altogether. To where the ghosts of little children go: that great, big, wonderful crèche in the sky.

I put the notebook I have been writing in away and look up at the now dazzling morning light. A small ray of sun is struggling to pierce the clouds and the effect of it, this little piece of magic in the midst of a Parisian winter, is heartening. It feels like a sign.

I remember reading that Sofia Coppola frequented the Luxembourg Gardens during the filming of *Marie Antoinette* and told a *New York Times* journalist that the beauty of this garden would always reassure her. Paris, she said, 'has a way of restoring your faith'.

I quietly whisper that I feel the same way.

I stand, confident that I can face any small ghosts who care to scamper across my path, and head for the Café de Flore, for a decadent breakfast of brioche and hot chocolate. There is nothing like a feast at the Café de Flore to make you feel that Paris is worth living in again. Winter may be here but it doesn't mean we have to let the cold into our hearts.

I walk towards the gates of the park—towards the promise of a new life.

For generations of expats, Paris has been the place where you come to find something—inspiration, adventure, a love affair, or simply a new talent. People think that filling their eyes with Paris will somehow also fill the emptiness in their lives, their relationships, or their careers. Well, sometimes it doesn't. Paris is the answer to many things but it is not the ultimate elixir. It can, however, take your mind of things for a little while, and give you hope for the future again.

. 13 .

La Vie Parisienne

FROM EXPAT TO INSIDER

*Paris is one of the most beautiful places in the world.
Unfortunately, I was so homesick I couldn't appreciate it.*

Tyra Banks

As most expats know, foreign cities can be unsettling places sometimes. There is the thrill of the novel, the new and the unknown, of course, which lasts for several months, or longer if you're lucky. But there are also the fears—the unspoken and profound fears—of loneliness, homesickness and cultural barriers difficult to overcome, from language problems to the challenge of finding good new foods. (When a girlfriend first arrived in Paris, the most intimidating thing about the city, she said, was the endless yoghurt aisles in the supermarkets.) Even those blessed with a sociable personality and an ability to make friends faster than a Frenchman can light a cigarette can feel the dread and trepidation that comes from being in a strange place far away from family, friends and familiar haunts.

This fear and loneliness is particularly strong around Christmas,

New Year's Eve and wintertime, when everyone heads home to their own families for a festive feast and a mid-winter rest. It's hard being an expat far from home at the best of times, but being alone far from home during the festive season can feel more isolating than being stuck in an Antarctic outstation on New Year's Eve with half a sparkler and a wet match.

What is interesting is that Parisians are now also starting to feel the isolation of urban living. Cities can be wonderful for preserving anonymity and privacy but they can also be alienating for the same reason, and Paris has the tendency to be particularly unfriendly. Parisians are known for their hauteur, and this, combined with their propensity to keep the best parts of the city to themselves—from great restaurants and bistros to the most beautiful places to buy shoes— means that infiltrating the chilly barriers of Parisian society, whether you've been here for five days or five years, can sometimes be a little difficult. Even New Yorkers are happy to recommend a great place to buy good bagels. And Londoners, while famously reserved (unless you went to school with their brother at Oxford or worked in the same City-based merchant bank as their cousin Tom), will always be happy to point you in the direction of a great pub.

The Parisian hauteur has become so prevalent in recent years that the city's more sociable sets are now trying to dampen the increasing chill by initiating a kind of 'learn how to be friendly' campaign. Part of this involves, well, being friendlier, especially to tourists (which is, admittedly working: being in Paris now is easier than in the days when waiters spilled coffee over you for badly spoken French). And part of it involves simply being nicer to your neighbour. Parisians are famously aloof when it comes to befriending those who live next door let alone around the corner, hence the establishment of a get-to-know-your-neighbours program.

The scheme, called *Peuplade* (which roughly translates as 'Tribe'), has been marketed with great fanfare, and certainly the idea has merit. The basic idea is 'to cross boundaries as well as boulevards'. By doing so Parisians will, it is hoped, begin not only to connect and acquaint themselves with the people who live around them, but also come to know an entirely different social set than the one they're used to mingling with. So if, for example, you're a stylish, well-dressed Left Banker with a penchant for Krug and *les honnêtes hommes* or a *mauvais garçon* (bad boy), it will introduce you to, say, a scruffily dressed, bohemian Canal St-Martin sort with an affinity for strong liquor and sexy, slightly naughty St-Germain women. So far, the scheme has had mixed results. As Simone puts it, it 'creates links between people who never really meet, and perhaps shouldn't do so'.

Quite a number of the world's media outlets have picked up on the initiative, which is often discussed at great lengths in Parisian newspaper columns. (Parisians themselves are alternately thrilled and insulted that they should need such a scheme: some feel it is a long time coming; others believe that French formality is there for a very good reason.) Jérémie Chouraqui, one of the founders of *Peuplade*, is a worthy advocate of the campaign.

'In life today we get to meet people in a very specific situation and social background,' he said to one journalist, '[but] with *Peuplade* you meet people that you would usually not get to meet: people with different ages and social backgrounds but who all live in the same neighbourhood.'

The scheme, he went on to explain, is based on a kind of electronic noticeboard: you log onto the website, scan your neighbourhood—or somewhere you want to become familiar with—and *voila!* The screen is (hopefully) full of potential candidates for a coffee and a chat.

Now I have been dying to test out the website. I have been dying to log onto the 'Apéro de Quartier', which gives you the opportunity to meet other friendly locals at a predetermined neighbourhood watering hole, and head off gaily to chat about, say other not-so-friendly locals and neighbours, over a wine or three well into the night. But so far I have been too shy to suggest a gathering of St-Sulpicers at the Café de la Mairie. And so have many others it seems. At the time of writing, some of the 'noticeboards' offering places and people to meet for a chat and a nice glass of red remain alarmingly blank. As one of my neighbours said the other day, 'We don't really want to meet any more people. We already have enough friends.' And she was one of the friendly locals.

As a social experiment, though, *Peuplade* is certainly an interesting one. After all, how do you get to meet your neighbours nowadays? It's too rude and unParisian to say *bonjour* when you stumble home from Le Fumoir at midnight, and it's not like you can invite them over for a barbecue like you do in Australia. Parisians are a fussy lot, and most of them wouldn't like the idea of some gauche stranger with bad taste messing up their well-ordered décor with a whole lot of nasty lamb chops and some ill-conceived salad leaves.

It will be interesting to see if *Peuplade* really does have any effect on the city's famously formal denizens. Personally, I think it may take a couple of centuries to break down the famous Parisian reserve. People here like to be a little haughty. (Of course, with their style and innate good taste, they have every reason to be.) But despite my fears, I wish the *Peuplade* people the best of luck. Anything that brings together Parisians is a fine initiative, in my opinion. Bring on the love-in.

Like many expats who find themselves living in a foreign city far from home, I have been surprised by the fact that I haven't made dozens of friends. (Although, after reading about *Peuplade*, I'm not so shocked now.) I thought—perhaps with a certain naivety—that I would have been drowning in new French friends by now, or at least paddling in the shallows with them. I thought that I would have had lots of lovely invitations to coffees and parties and teas and things, and maybe even a few saucy afternoon *rendez-vous* too. But the party invites have been scarcer than affordable Chanel and the saucy afternoon *rendez-vous* have been drier than a bad Bordeaux.

I thought I might have been 'in' with Lynton at least, and for a fleeting second did guilelessly assume I was heading for a fling with the womanising architect with a penchant for curves, caviar and Le Corbusier (my type of man). But his taste seems to veer more towards the 'rich and sexy Parisian sort' rather than the 'poor, gauche Australian girl' (surprising, really), so I've given up the idea of lazing in Lynton's penthouse pad wearing nothing but Sabbia Rosa and a smile.

I also thought I had a chance—although I think I knew it was a long shot, deep down in my heart—with Eric, the arse-loving Frenchman, but he is still too wrapped up in his Swedish sous chef, so I've given that dream away as well.

Basically, my love life is emptier than the shelves of Christian Louboutin at sales time. So much for my dreams of a Parisian-style romance in the courtyards of the Left Bank. Just as well I've come to realise that life is about far more than just a fervent French love affair.

If I was going to be truly honest with myself, however, I would admit, albeit only under the loosening powers of a Krug or two, that occasionally I feel bereft that my social life (forget the love life, which is obviously a lost cause) isn't on a par with my previous lives in Australia and London. I feel sad that I'm not quite at that 'best friends' stage with my Parisian acquaintances yet, even though I know I do have their love and support. And I wonder if I will ever truly fit in with Parisian society, despite being fortunate to have collected a handful of wonderful friends who are happy to dish up friendly advice on life and style and pause from their obviously frantic schedules to have a drink and chat with a sometimes crazy but mostly gracious Australian.

This quiet distress is one of the reasons why expats tend to

Edmonde Charles-Roux

CHANEL

Axel Madsen

CHANEL

ALICE
RAWSTHO

*Yves
Sain
Laurent*

A BIOGRAP

congregate with other expats after a certain length of time in Paris, and indeed most cities, if only for a bit of English language relief. With other foreigners, you can talk openly about the problems that present themselves living in a strange place. In the case of expats living in Paris, you can laugh about the neighbours making love all hours of the day and night with French fanfare (*Ah! Jean! Encore! Encore!*), while you sink further and further under your French franc–thin eiderdown, pouring increasingly larger glasses of cheap wine and emptying one foie gras dish after another onto a packet of crackers while watching old DVDs of *Sex and the City* or *Grey's Anatomy* and feeling supremely sorry for yourself. You can joke about the time you were invited to a party for grown-up singles and left after five minutes, whispering that you needed to find the powder room—in the bar down the street. You can talk about how your liver has exploded since you've come to Paris and is now begging you to take it to some kind of detox camp, preferably one in a warmer climate with lots of palm trees and no champagne in sight. You can talk about your addition to kir royals and your new propensity for diet pills (the Parisian woman's closely guarded slimming secret). And you can feel sympathy when someone tells you a story of how they once asked a work colleague for a recommendation of a great place to eat and the colleague directed them to a dodgy bistro with lukewarm food and chilly service, and when the person walked home afterwards they noticed the colleague in a far better establishment up the street, laughing with the owner and obviously emptying the fine cellar of its very best vintages. (Lesson: Parisians do not divulge their favourite *troquets* easily.) And lastly, you can laugh about your new French attitude, which tends to manifest itself in the *boulangerie* when old Madame Bouquet spends five hours flirting with the *boulanger* before deciding which cake she'll buy to feed her silly dog.

Ah yes, an expat's gathering can be a fulfilling event, full of reassuring conversations and lots of heartening laughs. (I once went to an expat party with the theme *'C'est normal'*, which is what everyone says in Paris. We had to come as something quintessentially French. I grabbed an empty wine glass and went as an expat. As Hemingway wrote in *The Sun Also Rises*: 'You're an expatriate ... fake European standards have ruined you. You drink yourself to death. You become obsessed by sex. You spend all your time talking, not working ... [and hanging] around cafés.')

But an expat get-together can also be wonderful for swapping fond memories of living in the city you now love, and (in the case of Paris) exchanging information on the best bits of this fabulous place and its distinctive, inimitable experiences. Some foreigners may occasionally complain about the service, the hauteur, the intimidating style that seems to be innate here (the first time you receive a 'French stare', where Parisians judge you on what you wear, is a truly daunting moment for a foreigner in Paris). But by and large, most foreigners feel a deep fondness for this most distinguished of destinations. They romanticise it before they come and then, after a length of time here, begin to romanticise it all over again, usually when they're out walking in a quiet street one Sunday morning, look up at the architecture, and realise they're living in a black and white postcard. They relish the light and the bridges and the sheer prettiness of the city, and even the laneways and their agonising cobblestones that threaten to wreck their new sky-high Louboutin heels. They love the dusks and the pinkness that settles on the city after the sun has set, causing it to blush with endearing charm at the end of the day. And they adore its grandness and pompousness and extraordinary good looks. They even love the quirky things about the city: the exotic, chaotic foodstalls of Belleville with the explicit produce and the way elegant boutiques like Sonia Rykiel offer finely crafted vibrators with the selection of well-cut business suits.

But mostly what my foreigner friends love are Paris's cafés, bars and bistros, where you can leave the elegant thoroughfares of the city for a brief moment and relish something as simple and delicious as a *chocolat à l'ancienne*—which, if you're lucky, comes with an enormous jug of thick melted chocolate, a smaller jug of perfectly steamed milk and a whole lot of fabulous French memories.

It is now the end of winter in Paris and as a fine mist of drizzle settles over the city for the umpteenth time, I have taken refuge from the season in what has become my favourite café—the Café de Flore. Here, as the warm lights glow, beckoning people inside, I listen to a philosophy discussion group (the members of which call themselves Café Philo) debating love and life in the City of Light. The stylish crowd makes me want to sit little straighter, gesture a little better and smile with delight at it all. It is Parisian inspiration at its very best.

This is my favourite time of day in Paris—*thé de cinq heures*, or five o'clock teatime. It is regarded as perhaps the most civilised time of day because you can step out of your routine to relax and catch up with a friend for a chat over a hot chocolate or a tea and a pastry or two. In fact, *le thé* is practically an institution in the city. Around five on weekends, somebody will invariably ask *'On fait le thé?'*

(Of course, tea and hot chocolate are not the most beloved drinks in Paris. Coffee is the liquid that energises the city and provides its citizens with their major fuel source. In fact, coffee has been an integral part of the culture of Paris since Hemingway and Orwell wrote entire chapters over a good, strong mind-blowing *corretto*—coffee with a dash of spirits. T.S. Eliot wrote to a friend that 'the chief danger about Paris is that it is such a strong stimulant'. But note, only foreigners drink *café crème* or *café au lait*, especially after lunchtime. If you want to be cool, go for a *café bio*, which uses coffee grown without pesticides and fertiliser. Very PC. Very Parisian.)

While the Café de Flore is one of the best places to drink any kind of hot drink, alcoholic or not, it is not the best place to indulge in that enchanting ritual known as *thé de cinq heures*. Ladurée is far more fitting for a gossip over a cup and saucer and a decadent macaroon or two. Flore is more for people watching—for hanging out with the publishing, literary and fashion crowds and feeling very *parisienne*. As Yves Saint Laurent's muse, Loulou de la Falaise, says (it is one of her favourite places): 'People like to make an entrance here.' The gorgeous Flore may proffer only a few types of tea but it offers all kinds of people watching. In fact, few come here for the cakes and pastries: it's customers fill up on the celebrities instead. Ladurée, on the other hand, is a small, sugar-coated slice of Paris society. Part tearoom, part gallery and part catwalk drama, it combines exquisite French design with old-fashioned flavours and classic Paris conversations. Everyone drops by here to pick up coffee and swap gossip between three and six.

I have to admit that, while I love the Flore with a passion, I will always have a soft spot for the quirky elegance of Ladurée. Jean-Louis told me when I first came to Paris that I needed to find a café to make my own. I needed to search out and identify a place where I could feel at home; a private low-key place to while away the day. Nearly every Parisian has one, he said. It was part of being *parisienne*.

I may have found my favourite place in the Café de Flore, but I think it may run equal with Ladurée. There is nothing, no problem or issue, you cannot solve with an hour of idling under the enchanting ceilings of its magnificent Left Bank salon. Other places may have better menus, more efficient service, even more memorable drinks. But there is something quintessentially Parisian about the quiet style of this overwhelmingly beautiful place. It almost epitomises the city in a way. Give me a pale green box any day.

Looking back over my time in Paris, I think it is these things—Ladurée, lingering in Left Bank cafés, learning to love life without children, or a spectacular career, or a staggeringly big house with ten bathrooms in the suburbs—that have come to define my time here. It has been an extraordinary period of personal growth, and it hasn't needed a man, or a French-style romance, or even the support of an enormous circle of friends (although a handful have kept the humour flowing). All it has required is Paris.

The past is another country, as the saying goes. The future is here to be lived. Pass me a glass of champagne. I'm ready to celebrate.

. 14 .

Au Revoir

You can't escape the past in Paris, and yet what's so
wonderful about it is that the past and present intermingle
so intangibly that it doesn't seem to burden.

Allen Ginsberg

It is springtime in Paris. The first leaves are starting to appear on the trees lining the Seine, delicious white asparagus is being featured on the city's best menus, the light over the city has changed from a wintry grey to a silvery, almost velvety shade and there is a joyous energy in the air as residents rediscover their spirit and famous *joie de vivre*. You almost feel like singing 'I love Paris in the springtime' as you stroll the streets of St-Germain.

No city was ever so associated with a season as Paris is with spring. It is a pairing of two perfect partners. Together, they offer possibility, potential, promise.

As I feel the warm days shake me out of my winter melancholy, assisted by long, slow strolls down the chestnut-lined avenues of this truly graceful place, I begin to think that there is no greater destination in which to lose yourself for a little while than the beautiful, bewitching boulevards of this magic metropolis. I have to leave here for a short while, to work elsewhere, but I know I will be back. I am sure of it. In a world of uncertainty there is one thing I know: Paris is part of my heart.

There is a thin mist the evening I leave and Paris feels snug under the blanket of it. The streetlamps seem huge in the thick soupy air, glowing like props on a grand stage, and as we drive down the wet black streets it seems as though all the lights of the city are reflected in the Seine.

The taxi driver, a glamorous black woman with a fur coat and a Louis Vuitton bag, which she leaves happily on the front seat, chats to me in French as we weave through the narrow streets. She mistakes me for a tourist and points out the Louvre, the Pyramid, the direction of the Palais Royale—the whole glorious lustre of it all.

I simply nod, not feeling brave enough to open my mouth in case I start to cry. I can't look at the city without feeling forlorn.

Then she realises I may be English and regards me in the rear-vision mirror.

'Holiday?' she says politely, smiling.

'*Oui*,' I lie, not wishing to tell her of a story that began with Henry Miller and doorways and finished with hope in my heart.

'Did you have a good time?' she asks, beaming again.

'*Oui*,' I say, smiling back at her with gratitude. 'I did, indeed.'